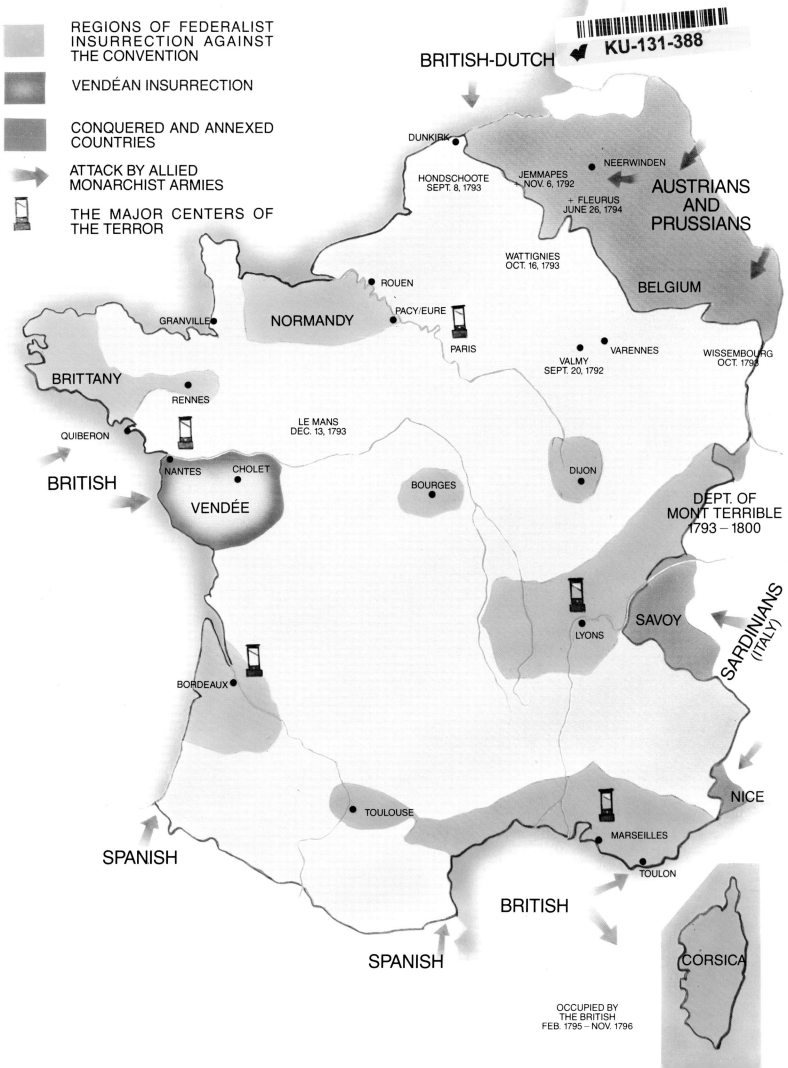

REGIONS OF FEDERALIST
INSURRECTION AGAINST
THE CONVENTION

VENDÉAN INSURRECTION

CONQUERED AND ANNEXED
COUNTRIES

ATTACK BY ALLIED
MONARCHIST ARMIES

THE MAJOR CENTERS OF
THE TERROR

BRITISH-DUTCH

DUNKIRK

HONDSCHOOTE
SEPT. 8, 1793

JEMMAPES
+ NOV. 6, 1792

NEERWINDEN

AUSTRIANS
AND
PRUSSIANS

+ FLEURUS
JUNE 26, 1794

WATTIGNIES
OCT. 16, 1793

BELGIUM

ROUEN

NORMANDY

PACY/EURE

PARIS

VALMY
SEPT. 20, 1792

VARENNES

WISSEMBOURG
OCT. 1793

GRANVILLE

BRITTANY

RENNES

LE MANS
DEC. 13, 1793

DIJON

QUIBERON

BRITISH

NANTES

CHOLET

VENDÉE

BOURGES

DEPT. OF
MONT TERRIBLE
1793 – 1800

LYONS

SAVOY

SARDINIANS
(ITALY)

BORDEAUX

NICE

TOULOUSE

SPANISH

MARSEILLES

BRITISH

TOULON

SPANISH

CORSICA

OCCUPIED BY
THE BRITISH
FEB. 1795 – NOV. 1796

CONTENTS

Published by Evans Brothers Limited
2A Portman Mansions
Chiltern Street
London W1M 1LE

First published in Great Britain in 1989 by Hamish Hamilton
Children's Books

Copyright © 1984 Casterman, originally published in French
under the title Les Jours de l'Histoire: La Révolution Française

Reprinted 1991, 1993

English translation copyright © Silver Burdett Press

Published by agreement with Casterman, Belgium

Printed in Hong Kong by Dah Hua Printing Co., Ltd

ISBN 0 237 60269 5

THE FRENCH
REVOLUTION

Hervé Luxardo
English translation by Nan Buranelli
Illustrations by Michael Welply

Evans Brothers Limited

"The Finest Kingdom on Earth"

Paris
September 15, 1787

My dear friend,

It has now been a year since I left London and set foot in the rich and powerful kingdom of France. How many people there are! France, with twenty-five million inhabitants, is in some ways the China of Europe. I have just dined with eight merchants who were returning from the fair at Beaucaire. We had traveled together, and I learned many things from their conversation.

Just think! The manufacturing industries emerged in about 1750. The textiles industry is, of course, the oldest and most important of them. Thanks to the new English machines and financial help from the state, cotton production in France has grown rapidly. Even so, to master the modern techniques, the mills here have been forced to send spies to England! I was informed that a certain John Holker founded a velveteen factory at Rouen by bribing about twenty English workers and stealing the design for the spinning frames! At Louviers different jennies (cotton-spinning machines) make it possible for one young girl to do the work of forty-six spinners. Such rapidity of execution means that eighteen thousand dozen pairs of stockings and bonnets can be produced at Rouen yearly.

Metallurgy, too, provides work for thousands in the Ardennes and in Franche-Comté. In Alsace the mills belonging to Dietrich, the Iron King, employ nearly a thousand workers. While visiting some factories, I was surprised to see children of six working there. And what are we to think of the wage scales, which are different from one place to another? At Beauvais, men earn forty sous to one hundred sous, but Breton weavers earn less than five sous for ten hours of work; bread alone costs

three sous a pound. And where would industry be without roads? Trudaine, the director of the *ponts et chaussées* [highway department], has renewed and extended the road system by 3,000 leagues [about 9,000 miles]. Since paving has been laid, travel is faster. Yet everything is relative. It took me sixteen hours to cover 20 leagues [about 60 miles]. With that said, it is better not to attempt the country roads; a French friend told me that the paths of hell could not be worse! However, that's not for want of calling on requisitioned peasant labor in Brittany for thirty, forty, or even fifty days of labor a year. These peasants are forced to leave their fields and toil twelve hours a day on the roads far from their homes. But the work is not accomplished without a struggle! In one place a foreman may drag them by the hair; elsewhere the peasants may simply refuse to work.

This is all to show you, my friend, how prosperity and misery walk side by side. Some villages I have been through are just heaps of rubble and dung. Near Guingamp in Brittany, I even thought I was in some strange land because the villagers knew so little French. The dwellings of the poor are just miserable mud huts without windows and almost without light. Two weeks ago I stopped at Montadier, a village in Languedoc situated on a steep mountainside covered with woods and lavender. In the village there are real beggars and an inn that made me almost recoil. Men with the look of cutthroats were eating black bread, and their faces spoke so eloquently of the galleys that I thought I could hear the sound of their chains. . . .

I shall continue, if it pleases you, to inform you of my impressions, which are certainly contradictory!

Your devoted Arthur.

Village Life

It is a Sunday morning in May 1780, and the leaves of the elm tree that spreads its branches over the village square of Nouans are trembling in the breeze. The clear sound of the church bells announces the end of the service, and the doors open for the crowd of worshipers. Peasant women, their heads covered in gray cloth, start for home; some are barefoot, but others wear stockings of blue wool and clack their wooden shoes. Meanwhile, the men, punctuating their lively conversation with many gestures, seat themselves on benches under the shade of the majestic elm.

As it does on most Sundays, the village community is meeting to discuss public matters. Master William, a rich farmer and procurator for the village, is in charge of the meeting. A collector of the *taille* (a tax levied by the king) must be appointed, and a new communal shepherd chosen. The shepherd, elected by a unanimous show of hands, is quickly found; a contract is made with Follet, a poor peasant whose crops were bad the year before. Every morning at daybreak he must assemble all the inhabitants' flocks and take them to pasture on the communal meadows or on the fallow lands, the farmlands that are allowed to rest one year in three. In summer, after the harvest, the shepherd will take the flocks to the seigneur's land, following a user's right that was won long ago. But choosing a tax collector, whose unpopular tasks appeal to no one, takes time and provokes lively discussion. Everyone avoids the duty, for good reason. If, for whatever reason, someone cannot pay the tax, the debt must be settled by the collector—under penalty of imprisonment!

In the months that follow, many other problems will be debated. The upkeep of the roads, and of the litter-filled streets that are often churned up by the rains, must be supervised. The nave of the church must be kept in order, the cemetery fencing must be repaired, and the feast for Saint Michael's Day must be organized. But when it is time to choose young men to be sent to the militia (the royal army) volunteers do not trample each other under the elm tree. Giving one's son to the army means losing the use of his hands for work on the farm.

Here, as elsewhere, a teacher is appointed each year, for since 1698 the opening of a school in every parish has been mandatory. A messenger is also appointed to take the mail to the nearest town. This messenger will be reimbursed by the villagers, either in money or in gifts of wheat sheaves. A midwife is chosen, too, and a doctor is contracted to look after the poor at no charge.

The Harvest Proclamation

Throughout the kingdom, just as here in Nouans, field work is always done communally. The date of the proclamation (the day the harvesting begins) is fixed each year. All the peasants are expected to answer the call to the general harvest and to the wine harvest. Beware, those who do not conform! In 1774, thirty-eight wine growers from the Côtes de Pommard were subjected to a forty-two-pound fine for having begun the harvest twenty-four hours too soon. In Burgundy the day of the proclamation is announced by the sound of trumpets, and processions are organized to chase the mice from the fields. To protect the crops, boxwood that has been blessed by the *curé* ("parish priest") is placed in the fields, on the doors of stables, and in cow sheds. When the harvest is in, the poor rush to glean the straw and ears of corn that have escaped the harvesters. In the autumn, after the fields have been worked, bundles of firewood are prepared in anticipation of winter.

Since the middle of the eighteenth century, many French writers and philosophers have made the English way of life fashionable. For some aristocrats this manifests itself in their choosing to withdraw from court life to live on their lands and modernize their properties. The bourgeoisie adopt tea, which the English have sent from their Indian colonies, as their favorite drink. Thé à l'Anglaise "tea in the English manner," becomes a ceremony in their salons.

But along with English fashions, the idea of revolution is taken up by the bourgeoisie. Did not the English depose their king, James II, in 1688? Did they not cut off Charles I's head in 1649?

The Bourgeoisie in the City

They are strange to watch, these well-to-do citizens rushing around Paris. At about ten o'clock in the morning, a black cloud of judges and lawyers makes its way to the Châtelet. At noon the stockbrokers crowd into the Exchange and the stockholders retire to the gardens of the Palais-Royal. At two o'clock all the cabs are besieged, and it is not unusual for two doctors to open the doors of one of them at the same time and for both to climb in. A dispute will inevitably follow. At five o'clock it is time for a show or a walk, and the cafés fill up.

The luxury of the richest bourgeois dwellings indicates success in business. At the home of Monsieur Beaujon, in the Champs-Elysées, a stairway of exotic wood and a table that seats thirty are the pride of the household. "People of quality" fight for invitations from the farmers-general. The wealthiest of all the bourgeoisie, these financiers number only forty in the entire kingdom. They lend the king considerable sums and have earned the right to reimburse themselves by levying indirect taxes.

"The ladies of the court," so it is said, "are very jealous, not only of the beauty and success of their wives but also, and above all, of the luxurious surroundings in which they live." Not one of these bourgeoisie would want to miss a meeting in the salons of Madame d'Epinay or Madame Geoffrin. At the salon of Julie Talma, the guests hold their discussions in Roman-style surroundings, for the ancient Roman Republic is considered fashionable. Counselors, or men of law, and journalists or newswriters, come to deliver brilliant lectures. It is here that men who will soon be famous, such as Camille Desmoulins, Jacques Brissot, Pierre Vergniaud, Pierre-Roger Ducos are encountered.

In bourgeois homes, pictures of rural or family scenes decorate the walls. In their libraries, the pride and joy of their owners, the books that are in fashion and that are good form to discuss, are collected. Just like some aristocrats, the bourgeoisie like to read and comment on philosophers' works that denounce injustice. None of them could afford to be ignorant of the writings of Montesquieu, Jean-Jacques Rousseau, and Voltaire or of Denis Diderot and Jean d'Alembert, chief editors of the *Encyclopédie*, published from 1751 to 1765. In the articles contained in twenty-seven volumes that have already appeared, the encyclopedia emphasizes the scientific knowledge and techniques of the era and questions royal absolutism.

Aware of their intellectual value and their economic power, these upper-middle-class citizens are men of progress and of culture. They are exasperated at having to pay taxes from which the clergy and the nobility, which spends its time ruining itself at court, are exempt. Although they are men of talent, the bourgeoisie realize that they are excluded from political power and that their sons are barred from military careers, which are reserved for the aristocracy. They also criticize absolute monarchy and the despotism of kings. They call themselves "men of the century of enlightenment" and favor economic progress and individual liberty. They admire English democracy and the United States Constitution of 1787. All of these bankers, merchants, factory owners, lawyers, and doctors, are making the country wealthy and desire to take part in political life.

Life at Court

A young nobleman, Monsieur de Chateaubriand, who leads a peaceful existence on his lands in Brittany, has been invited to court at Versailles. What excitement! Versailles! Versailles means being presented to the king; it means mixing with the highest aristocracy! It is this same aristocracy that from all accounts plots daily to secure positions in the royal administration. So de Chateaubriand will leave for Versailles; it will be a chance to have a brilliant career, since the king, Louis XVI, saves his grants and favors for those presented to him. Is it not true that the Duchess of Polignac received 800,000 livres for marrying off her daughter? The king also gives concessions for the exploitation of coal mines and for high ranks in the army.

The nobility's role is also to assist the king in every aspect of his private life. Four thousand aristocrats live at court. To be summoned to the king's levee (morning rising) is both an honor and an opportunity to be noticed. The gentlemen wait impatiently in the vast salon, called the *Oeil de Boeuf* ("Bull's-Eye"), for the king to emerge from his bedchamber. On the stroke of eleven-thirty a page shouts: "Gentlemen of the wardrobe!" Then the "princes of the blood" (those related to the king) slip into the chamber. The king's toilet begins; he puts on his shoes and shirt. When the king has only his coat to slip on, a page calls "The bedchamber." This is the moment when all the pages and their tutor, the chaplains, and the courtiers enter.

To maintain one's rank at court, one must be rich. A nobleman, who, so to speak, has no right to exercise a trade on pain of derogating or losing his title, is forced to raise his peasants' rents. He must also keep any privileges he has in force. Since 1781 a ruling has limited the rank of officer to aristocrats who can prove they have four ancestors of noble origin.

To replenish the state coffers, the monarchy had habitually sold noble ranks, such as those of secretaries of state, for a high price. In this way, a *noblesse de robe*, or "aristocracy of the gown," developed. It allied itself, by marriage, with the traditional aristocracy, called the aristocracy *d'épée*, or "of the sword," because they alone had the right to carry a sword. Under Louis XVI, however, the nobles seized all these positions. The aristocracy, more protective than ever of its privileges, prevented the middle class from achieving nobility and became a closed society. The disdain it showed toward a class that was richer and better educated than itself fanned jealousies and deeply rooted hatreds.

Until 1787 the king gave a ball every Wednesday for the queen. There the pages, who had to arrive first, waited to show the ladies to their seats and offer them refreshments. Nothing was left to chance. Two chambermaids were on duty in a dressing room to repair any costumes that might have been torn while dancing was in progress. At midnight, footmen served supper. The king appeared only to play trictrac but did not like the court to play for high stakes. Very rarely did he venture in an evening to lose more than two gold louis, which, after all, was a month's wages for a mason.

The Estates General

At the end of the Middle Ages, the king of France adopted the practice of consulting representatives from the nobility, the clergy, and the middle class in the cities. The sovereign retained his power but took into account the opinions of these subjects when making important decisions, especially with regard to taxes. He would call together delegates from the "three orders": the nobility, the clergy, and the Third Estate (the bourgeoisie of the towns and cities, and wealthy country farmers). Little by little it became customary for the three orders to elect deputies, who met during the main convention of the Estates General held in the king's presence. But the strengthening of royal power, especially under Louis XIV, allowed the king to stop summoning the Estates General, in which each order could give its opinion on the political situation and the administration of the country.

Incapable of estimating a budget in 1788, Louis XVI and his ministers had to con-

front a catastrophic situation. Expenditures for the army, the court, foreign affairs, road constructions and so on, far exceeded the income from taxes. To find money, the king resigned himself to asking the nobility and the clergy to pay taxes that they had escaped until then. Claiming that tradition protected them, these privileged classes refused to pay and demanded the convening of the Estates General. According to the privileged classes, only they could vote new contributions and taxes.

Jacques Necker, the controller general of finances, promised a meeting of the three orders for May 1789. As was customary for the occasion, they were allowed to draw up *cahiers de doléances,* or "memos of grievances," in which they could express their hopes, their complaints, and their proposals for reform.

Clinging to their privileges, most of the aristocracy stated in their memos that they "would never consent to the abolition of rights they had inherited from their ancestors." On the other hand, the members of the Third Estate wanted to abolish the seigneurial taxes and the ecclesiastical tithe

imposed on the bourgeoisie. They also wanted to share hunting rights that had been the nobility's preserve until then.

On May 5, 1789, the deputies of the three orders gathered at Versailles. They numbered 1,139, with 578 deputies representing the Third Estate. The king presided over the first sitting, and Necker made a long speech during which he never once uttered the word *reform.* The deputies of the Third Estate were all the more disappointed when the "vote by head count," one of their main requests, was not granted. If, as custom had established, the vote was by order, the clergy, the nobility, and the Third Estate would each have one vote. What good would that do for the deputies of the Third Estate, who were as numerous as the two other orders put together? The nobility and the clergy would certainly make their "privileged" point of view triumph.

Exasperated by the royal attitude as well as by the attitudes of the king's ministers, the deputies of the Third Estate decided on June 17 to no longer sit in session with the nobility and the clergy. Instead, since they represented "ninety-seven percent of the nation," they declared themselves a national assembly. The king refused to accept this brilliant maneuver and closed the hall where the deputies of the Third Estate were meeting. On June 20 the deputies installed themselves in the Tennis Court Hall and solemnly swore not to leave until they had established a constitution. Louis XVI eventually had to give in to the determination of the Third Estate. He ordered the deputies of the nobility and the clergy (some of whom had not waited for the king's decision) to unite with the Third Estate. He accepted the vote by head count and, on July 9, 1789, ratified the proclamation of the National Constituent Assembly.

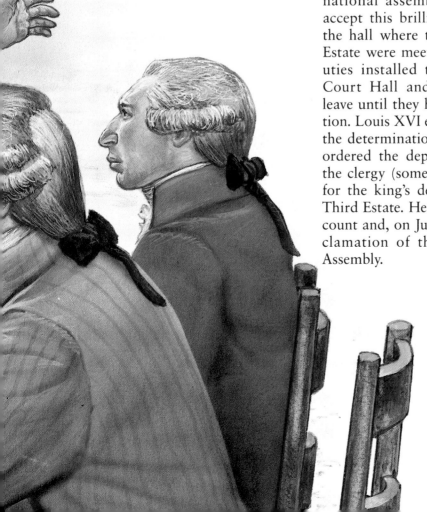

When the convocation of the Estates General was announced, the village community in each parish met to draw up its list of grievances. The complaints were many, but how to put them in order? Who would hold the pen? The schoolmaster? Could he write well enough?

It was not uncommon for a rich farmer to be able to send his son to college in the city. Having become a "gentleman"— perhaps a notary's clerk, a counselor, or a solicitor— the son would often return to the village for this solemn occasion and take on the responsibility of secretary. Cleverly, while paying attention to the claims of the peasants, he would succeed in imparting to the gathering the ideas he had heard promulgated by the bourgeoisie in the city. It is due to these educated people that we can find statements in the peasants' memos about liberty of the press, a constitution, and the separation of powers. Strictly speaking, these terms meant nothing to the peasants but were suggested to them at the right moment and were accepted because the peasants were told that everyone thought that way. . . .

Storming the Bastille!

At the end of June 1789, the movements of the king's thirty thousand troops, who were patrolling around Paris for the first time, made the population uneasy. All kinds of alarming rumors began to circulate. Wasn't it true that "the high clergy and the nobility" were plotting against the Third Estate and trying to "make a portion of the population die of starvation"? What about the so-called famine pact? The previous year, 1788, had been hard for the majority of the 650,000 Parisians, for the crops had been disastrous. Then, in the spring of 1789, storms and heavy rains came one after the other, and people knew that the wheat would be delivered late. The price of bread was too high. In just a few days it had gone from eight sols to twenty sols. Cabinetmakers and carpenters from the Faubourg St.-Antoine, cobblers and weavers from the Faubourg St.-Marcel, and fishwives from the Halles, who only earned about thirty sols per day, all muttered about the ministers and the bakers, accusing them of being "starvers of the people."

On Sunday, July 12, the announcement that Necker had been dismissed upset the

people of Paris. The minister of finance was believed to have opposed those who were buying up grain. To the Parisians it looked as if the king was preparing to dismiss the Assembly. At the Palais-Royal an aristocrat was beaten by some "patriots" for having spat at Necker's portrait. Some of the artillery men at the Invalides were rumored to have mutinied. The most respected orator at the Palais-Royal, Camille Desmoulins, stood on a table and harangued the crowd: "Now that they have forced out Necker, the privileged ones will do anything, and for tonight perhaps they are planning to massacre the patriots! To arms! Yes, it is I who summon my brothers to liberty!"

Mobs formed. Soon six thousand people were parading through Paris, preceded by a bust of Necker and black flags signifying mourning. In the Tuileries gardens the mob clashed with cavalry of the provincial regiments that had been called in. Stones and chairs rained down on the military. News of the brawl spread rapidly. Pillaging of the armories began at the same time. On July 13, the angry crowd, fearful of famine, attacked the forty gates in the wall where the Farmers-General taxed merchandise for the right of entry. The French guards joined the people and attacked the convent of St.-Lazare and the Halles, which had large quantities of food in storage. The people also seized the opportunity to break down the doors of the prisons and release the debtors who had been detained there.

In the arsenal, where arms were stored, people were disappointed to find that the gunpowder had already been transferred to the Bastille, and the guns, to the Invalides. Cries of treason arose! At the town hall the bourgeoisie then decided to create a Parisian militia or "national guard" of eight hundred men, as much to avoid a takeover from Versailles by the king's troops as to prevent the populace from pillaging. On the morning of July 14, a considerable crowd wearing cockades of red and blue, the colors of the city of Paris, invaded the Invalides and distributed the forty thousand guns and twelve cannons they found there. But the gunpowder and ammunition were at the Bastille.

On July 14, at ten o'clock in the morning, three men backed up by the crowd came to parley in front of the bars of the Bastille's gates. De Launay, governor of the fortress, allowed the three city deputies, among them the lawyer Thuriot, to enter. Thuriot asked the governor to remove the cannons from the tower and to come to terms with the people. De Launay agreed only to draw back the cannons from the ramparts.

Between noon and one o'clock, more crowds arrived "armed with picks, sabers, and axes." Someone succeeded in sliding along the chain of the little drawbridge at the advanced post that led to the outer courtyard. He lowered it. But the guards fired from inside and prevented him from letting down the second drawbridge.

At three o'clock in the afternoon, de Launay at last decided to lower the drawbridge. The crowd rushed into the courtyard, disarmed the 114 soldiers on duty, and threw the archives out the windows. One of the insurgents addressed the Bastille guards: "You have fired on your country—you deserve to be hanged, and you will be, immediately." Seven of the guards were massacred, and de Launay's head was cut off. The Bastille, where the king had been able to imprison anyone he wished with a simple *lettre de cachet,* or "sealed order," had fallen. For the patriots it meant the end of royal despotism.

The frightened king withdrew his troops from the capital and recalled Necker. On July 17, he recognized the Marquis de Lafayette, the popular hero of the American War for Independence, as the commander of the National Guard in Paris. At last the king accepted the tricolor cockade; the royal white added to the red and blue of the Parisians became the national colors.

Citizen Palloy's "Bastilles"

The fallen Bastille immediately became a very fashionable place to promenade. Some deputies of the Third Estate, including Mirabeau, dislodged stones from the wall and threw them from the top of one of the towers to signify the end of the old regime. Those who liked to experience strong emotions had themselves shut up in the evening in the old dungeons. . . . But there was one man— François Palloy, a masonry contractor—who understood completely the benefits to be had from the old fortress. As early as the evening of July 15, eight hundred of his workers were already at work on the Bastille. The demolition work was to go on until May 1791. In 1790, Palloy borrowed from one of his stonecutters the idea of carving little models of the Bastille from each stone. Thus thousands of little "Bastilles" were sent to all the communes of France. He himself built a house at Sceaux, in Hauts-de-Seine, with stones from the Bastille.

The Great Fear

After July 14, 1789, the roads of France were unusually busy. The carriages of the first aristocratic émigrés beginning to flee and the royal troops leaving the capital to go back to their garrisons made people apprehensive. The news from Paris arrived slowly. Were the aristocrats plotting against the Third Estate? Were the destitute-looking people who were in the fields everywhere bandits? Was the Revolution failing? Who should be believed? What should be believed?

Contradictory rumors ran from village to village, and the tocsins responded to each other dismally. In Auvergne the terrified population hid in the depths of the woods or in the recesses of caves and grottoes. Couriers rode at full speed around the countryside to tell anyone who would listen that everything had been plundered and burned. In the provinces where "the great fear" played havoc, the villagers armed themselves with pitchforks.

There were many reasons for these panics. In Soissonnais the fear had no origin other than the notions of five or six field hands who had gotten drunk and slept in the corn and were threatening to cut everything up. Disquiet spread. Just a few burning weeds or the sun reflected in the window of a château would make people think the crops were being burned, set on fire by brigands. A laborer going through the woods would think he saw bandits in the uncertain light of the moon. In general, the great fear lasted about twenty-four hours.

On the morning of July 28, at Nexon in the Limousin, a knave ran up crying "To arms, to arms!" He caught his breath, wiped his brow, and, breathing hard, related that a servant had told him that "ten thousand foreigners" were laying waste all over the country. All the men, equipped with halberds and harquebuses, met on the heights of the village, firmly determined to defend to the last their goods—and maybe their skins, too. But the night passed, and the men waited in vain, with no brigands in sight.

Once the initial panic was over, the peasants realized their strengths and turned against their overlords, who were accused of originating the great fear. In Isère several thousand peasants laid siege to castles, burned the seigneurial rent registers, and helped themselves to food and drink. Not only castles were burned, but many rich farms were burned, too. At Versailles the Constituent Assembly was thrown into a panic. On August 4 the bourgeois members and some broad-minded noblemen thought of a way to satisfy the peasants. The honorary seigneurial rights (carrying a sword, having a reserved seat in church, being first in processions, and so on), the tithe, and the corvée (unpaid labor, as on the roads) were abolished in a burst of general enthusiasm, for the sacrifice cost little. In return, to show that they did not wish to attack property, the bourgeois members of the Assembly, themselves owners of domains of which they were sometimes also seigneurs, decided that the rights burdening the lands, in particular the right of the seigneur to a portion of the crop, and smaller impositions, like having to grind their grain at the seigneur's mill, could be bought back by the peasants at thirty times their value!

On August 26 the Constituent Assembly solemnly published the Declaration of the Rights of Man and of the Citizen. This is how it summed up the great principles of 1789: "Ignorance, neglect, or disdain for the rights of man are the sole causes of the public misfortunes and of the corruption of governments. Man is born free and equal in rights." These rights are "liberty, property ownership, safety, and resistance to oppression," so that "no one has the right to be harassed because of his opinions." The law expressed of the general will that "any society in which the guarantee of rights is not assured, nor the separation of powers 'executive, legislative, and judiciary' laid down, has no constitution."

The old regime had just collapsed.

The castle is taken but there is still something to be accomplished. The peasants know just what they are looking for—the property register, a large register in which their seigneur has had a specialist from the neighboring town record all the rights he has been able to find in his archives, some of them dating back to the Middle Ages. The torn documents are thrown out of the windows and carried off by the wind. After this great day it will take a brave person to say what rights the peasants must pay for in the future!

The Days of October

On the morning after August 4, 1789, when seigneurial privileges were partly abolished, Louis XVI took up his pen and wrote: "I will never consent to robbing my clergy and nobility. I shall not sanction decrees (the Declaration of the Rights of Man, and the abolition of privileges) that rob them."

Nothing could compel Louis XVI to give his consent, all the more so because the Constituent Assembly was divided. One party of deputies, called monarchians, was in favor of ending the Revolution and giving the king the opportunity to reject the revolutionary laws. The majority of deputies opposed this idea but granted Louis XVI the right to veto, allowing him to refuse the application of any law he objected to.

On October 1 the officers of the Flanders Regiment gave a banquet for the king in the opera theater at the Palace of Versailles. The menu was extensive, and wine flowed like rivers. When the royal family appeared, the gentlemen turned their tricolor cockades inside out, turning them into cockades of white, the king's color. Cries of "Down with the Constituent Assembly!" were heard.

At the same time, in Paris "the horrors of famine are making themselves felt. Bakers' shops are besieged, the people lack bread." Patriotic newspapers stated that Versailles had not only insulted the nation by acclaiming the white cockade, but also was hoarding flour and, even worse, preparing a counterrevolution.

At dawn on October 5, a group of women decided to go to Versailles. Dressed in white, with their hair done up and powdered for the occasion, some of them dragged along any passerby they encountered. Supported by market porters from the Halles, to the beat of a drum, they broke into a gun shop. Five thousand to six thousand women set out to "cut the queen's head off," because she was reported to have said "If they don't have any bread, let them eat cake!" At noon the tocsins sounded in all the clock towers of

Paris. People, especially women, from the working class quarters assembled in front of the town hall, where, at the end of the afternoon, Lafayette, the commander of the National Guard, was welcomed with cries of "To Versailles! Give us bread! The government is deceiving us!" He, too, decided to go. A column of several thousand people and fifteen thousand national guardsmen then headed for Versailles.

It was pouring rain when the first of the women arrived within sight of the palace. Several hundred of them, chanting "Bread! Bread!" forced themselves into the Hôtel des Menus, where the Constituent Assembly was in session. In the palace the king heard the drums sounding the call to arms. Soon, four women accompanied by deputies from the Third Estate appeared. One of the women, overcome by emotion at the sight of the sovereign, had just time to murmur "Bread" before she fainted. But nothing actually happened until the following day.

In the morning a group of insurgents forced their way into the king's apartments. Two royal guards were beheaded. The besieged royal family was in a desper-ate situation. The king then decided to show himself on the balcony of the palace's Marble Court. He was met by cheers: "Long live the king! Let the king return to Paris!" The queen appeared next, with her son. She was jeered, and guns were aimed in her direction; fearful, she drew back. Lafayette had just arrived; he pulled her onto the balcony again and kissed her hand. Touched by this gesture, the crowd changed its attitude and cried "Long live the queen! Let the queen return to Paris!"

Then the procession, bristling with pikes, including two bearing the heads of the two massacred guards, set off to return to Paris. Carts full of wheat and flour pre-ceded the royal family's gilded carriage. "The baker, the baker's wife, and the baker's little boy," as the king, the queen, and their son were called, were from then on under the surveillance of the people of Paris.

The king was installed in his new apart-ments in the Tuileries. As for the Constitu-ent Assembly, it left Versailles for Paris and met in the riding school. Thus it responded to the people's wish to have the different authorities of the nation in their power.

The Festival of the Federation

For July 14, 1790, the first anniversary of the taking of the Bastille, the municipality of Paris decided to celebrate "the unification of the French people" with a grand ceremony. Every region in France was invited to send delegates from the National Guard of each department. Thousands of men started out from the eighty-three departments, which were created in 1790 to replace the old provinces. More than twenty thousand delegates arrived in Paris on July 12.

The Champ de Mars, an immense oval space, was surrounded by tiers of wooden seats. In the middle rose the Altar of the Nation. At the four corners of the altar were urns from which the smoke of incense drifted.

On the morning of July 14, 1790, a long procession left the Place de la Bastille for the Champ de Mars. At the head of the procession were the Parisian authorities and the deputies of the National Constituent Assembly. The unarmed soldiers of the old royal army followed, while the National Guards marched carrying guns or sabers. At noon the fifty thousand men of the army and the National Guard arrived at the Champ de Mars, to the applause of 400,000 spectators who had been waiting for them, stoically, in the rain. The king, the queen, and the dauphin (the royal couple's son), who had taken their places on a platform, were also applauded; Lafayette, arriving on a prancing white horse, received a tremendous ovation. At three o'clock, Charles-Maurice de Tallyrand-Perigord, the bishop of Autun, celebrated mass assisted by sixty chaplains and accompanied by the sound of drums and trumpets. He blessed the flags of the eighty-three departments. The sound of cannon fire rang out.

Lafayette then advanced and climbed the steps leading to the altar. On it he placed the point of his sword and made this pronouncement: "We swear to be ever faithful to the nation, the law, and the king." At the signal of a tricolor oriflamme (banner), the standard of the early kings of France, all the national guardsmen raised their hands and shouted: "I swear." Then it was the king's turn to take an oath, and he rose and assured the gathering that he would maintain the Constitution. The queen then participated in the "triumph of the nation," presenting her son, holding him out to the audience. Immediately, cries of "Vive le roi, vive la reine, vive le dauphin" (Long live the king, long live the queen, long live the prince) arose. Emotion was at a peak. In the evening the people of Paris danced on the ruins of the Bastille and on the illuminated Place Louis XV.

But the splendor of the festival in no way changed the divisions among the French

people. At the Constituent Assembly the aristocrats, who were seated to the right of the president of the session, defended their privileges inch by inch. The bourgeois deputies, seated on the left, tried to have significant rights granted to them in the new Constitution. Only a few democrats among them worried about the fate of the people and upheld the principle of universal suffrage, from which, however, they excluded women. The majority of the deputies were opposed to universal suffrage and decided to grant the right to vote only to "active citizens," those who paid three pounds of taxes a year; the others, called "passive citizens," did not receive any political rights.

But the lack of money and the bankruptcy of the state that had caused the summoning of the Estates General was not yet solved. To end the problem, the deputies nationalized the lands and certain other possessions of the clergy. Paper money in the form of *assignats*, or promissory notes, was issued to pay the functionaries and the suppliers of the state. These people could exchange their assignats for national property that was to be put up for sale. This was the first appearance of paper money in France.

Deputies of the Constituent Assembly began to meet away from the Assembly so that they could carry on their discussions. Some of the deputies founded a club in Paris; they met in the former monastery of the Jacobin (Dominican) friars, whose name the deputies kept. Soon they were joined by middle-class revolutionaries with a passionate interest in politics. From 1790 on, the Jacobin Club members founded popular societies in the provinces with which they associated themselves. In the same way, the *club des Cordeliers* gathered in the church of the Franciscan friars, but this club had a less affluent following than the Jacobins.

If the plan organized for the king's departure had been carried out, it would have set a record for speed in that era. Initially it had been calculated that with nineteen changes of horses, the royal coach could in one day traverse the 175 or so miles separating Paris from Montmédy, where the Marquis de Breteuil's army awaited it.

But the ordinary citizen traveled much more slowly. The diligence *("stagecoach") took four days to get to Lyons and nearly a week to reach Marseilles.*

The King's Flight

At the beginning of 1791, the Cordelier Club, founded by Georges-Jacques Danton, was openly criticizing not only the moderate attitude of the rich deputies of the Assembly, but also the ambiguous positions taken by the king. A fervent Catholic, Louis XVI was profoundly shocked by the suppression of the religious orders and by the Civil Constitution of the Clergy, which transformed priests and bishops, who were elected by the faithful, into functionaries of the state. The king approved of the refractory priests who opposed the "jurors," those who took the oath imposed by the Constituent Assembly: "To the nation, the law, and the king."

On April 18 the king wished to go to St.-Cloud to attend a mass celebrated by a nonjurist priest, but the crowd prevented him from going. Opposed in his convictions and disapproving of the revolu-

tionary measures that had been taken, he decided to flee abroad, where he hoped to join other nobles who had emigrated for fear of the Revolution, a number of whom were living along the Rhine River at Koblenz. They believed they would be able to draw all the European sovereigns into a counterrevolutionary crusade.

Everything was ready on the evening of June 20. At midnight a heavy coach left with the royal couple and their children for Montmédy, in Meuse, 175 miles from the capital. The king wore the livery of a valet in the service of Baroness Korff, the name the queen had assumed. But the coach lost time; the king, who liked to be comfortable, ordered more and more stops to stretch his limbs. When they arrived at Chàlons, it was already four o'clock in the morning. None of the patrols that were to escort the carriage were in sight. Tired of waiting, they had abandoned their posts. The coach continued on unescorted. . . .

In a cloud of dust, and with a great deal of noise, the coach rolled into Ste.-Men-

ehould, followed by peasants returning from the fields. Among them, Drouet, son of the postmaster, racked his memory. Where could he have seen this stout man before, in his valet's livery, leaning on his arm at the window of the carriage? Drouet ran to warn the municipality of his suspicions, but it was too late—the coach had already left. With his friend, William, he jumped on horseback and pursued the coach at full speed. At Varennes the king lost more time locating fresh horses. Meanwhile, Drouet and William arrived and roused the population, which crowded around the carriage. It was the end of the journey.

At dawn on June 22 the royal carriage returned to Paris, surrounded by six thousand national guardsmen and several thousand peasants. The Constituent Assembly, which still wanted to have a king, tried to convince the people that he had been kidnapped. The Assembly had notices plastered on the walls of the capital on which could be read:

"Whoever applauds the king will be beaten, whoever insults him will be hanged . . ." The people, who were not deceived, welcomed their monarch with dead silence on June 25.

Danton and the Cordeliers demanded that a republic be proclaimed and the king be put on trial. On Sunday, July 17, 1791, they deposited a petition to this effect on the Altar of the Nation at the Champ de Mars. Fearing a riot against the king and the Constituent Assembly, Lafayette and the mayor of Paris decreed martial law and fired on the people; fifty people were killed and hundreds more were wounded.

Abroad, these events aroused some anxiety. On August 27, 1791, the emperor of Austria and the king of Prussia threatened to intervene if the king was attacked physically. On September 30 the Constituent Assembly split up and the Legislative Assembly took over.

The Fall of the Monarchy

In the autumn of 1791, the active citizens elected 745 deputies to the Legislative Assembly. The moderates were in the majority. On the left were the Girondists, who owed their name to the fact that their most brilliant orators had been elected in Gironde and who hoped to spread the Revolution throughout Europe, delivering it from "the tyranny of monarchs."

For his part, the king wanted a war that he hoped to lose so that the foreign armies could restore the old regime. He chose, therefore, in the spring of 1792 to dismiss those ministers who were too pacifistic and to replace them with Girondists. On April 20, despite the warnings of Maximilien de Robespierre, a young lawyer from Arras who alerted the Jacobin Club to the dangers of such an adventure, the Legislative Assembly voted to declare war on Austria, which had threatened France with reprisals if anyone harmed the king.

Louis XVI was jubilant: "Instead of a civil war, we shall have a political war. The state of France is such that it cannot possibly sustain a partial campaign." The queen, Marie Antoinette, sister of the Austrian emperor, was even more specific: "The idiots, they do not see that this will be to our advantage."

In Paris the passive citizens—those deprived of the right to vote—made up their minds to take a part in political activity to defend and continue the Revolution. They held assemblies in each of the forty-eight districts of the city. In these gatherings the *sansculottes* (a name chosen by them because they wore trousers, not the breeches that were fashionable during the old regime) discussed events and stored arms in anticipation of a struggle.

Using his right of veto, the king opposed the measures taken by the Legislative Assembly. He rejected the decrees against the refractory priests and, particularly, the call to Paris of twenty thousand provincial national guardsmen, who were to be installed in a camp on the Champ de Mars to defend the capital.

Toward noon, on June 20, a crowd of sansculottes erupted into the château of the Tuileries to make the king yield. He agreed to receive them, put on a red cap, and toasted the nation, but he maintained his veto. The Girondists and Robespierre ignored him. The twenty thousand national guardsmen were summoned for July 14.

Those arriving from Marseilles sang a marching song that a young officer, Rouget de Lisle, had composed for the army of the Rhine. For all the Parisians this war song was to become "La Marseillaise."

By July 28, alarming news was circulating: Charles Brunswick, a Prussian general, had published a manifesto threatening Paris with military destruction. Convinced that the king had betrayed them, forty-seven of the forty-eight districts demanded his deposition.

Robespierre prepared a plot, the date of which was fixed for August 10. On the morning of the great day, Danton and his friends seized the town hall and installed the Insurrectional Commune. A thousand or so sansculottes tried to get into the Tuileries. But the accurate fire of the Swiss grenadiers and some gentlemen from the windows stopped half of the assailants short.

But a second assault wave, this time accompanied by the National Guard and its cannon, silenced the defenders in a hail of shot. Fourteen thousand attackers plunged into the château, and to the sound of "La Marseillaise" they massacred nearly two thousand of its occupants.

The king and his family had left the Tuileries and taken refuge with the Legislative Assembly. The deputies, under the threat of the cannons, voted the king's deposition.

He was taken immediately to the Temple prison. The deputies established universal suffrage for men and decided to call a new assembly: the National Convention.

Until new elections were held, the Insurrectional Commune was in power. But the news of the invasion of Lorraine by the Prussians moved the people of Paris, still intoxicated by the gunpowder and blood of August 10, to violence. The sansculottes were convinced that the city was a nest of royalist spies who were just waiting for the volunteers to leave for the front so that they could unleash a counterrevolution. From September 2 to September 8, small groups of people armed with clubs, swords, and axes had those prisoners who had been held in the principal Parisian prisons turned over to them. After a mere semblance of justice before an improvised tribunal, they bludgeoned and executed their victims. In all, thirteen hundred people—among them some nobles and refractory priests but mainly common-law prisoners—were put to death.

To prevent such uncontrolled massacres, Danton, the minister of justice, decided to create the first Revolutionary Tribunal.

The war, the appearance of the sansculottes on the scene, and the insurrection of August 10 had pushed the Revolution into its most violent phase.

At nine-thirty on the morning of August 10, the sansculottes of Paris, singing "La Marseillaise" and marching elbow to elbow, made a victorious assault on the Tuileries and swept out the monarchy.

The War

To defend the frontiers against the Austrian and Prussian armies, the Legislative Assembly, mistrusting the regiments of the line, whose aristocratic officers were generally in favor of the old regime, had to appeal to the volunteers of the National Guard. On July 22 the Assembly declared, "The country is in danger!" The situation was frenzied. Everyone wanted to march immediately on the enemy. In Paris, ten thousand volunteers joined up in one day. Some women even pushed patriotic ardor so far as to disguise themselves as men so that they could enlist! On July 30 a decree finally authorized passive citizens to join the National Guard. In this way a fair number of sansculottes were able to rejoin the army.

These new recruits elected their own officers and could leave the army after each campaign. Poorly equipped, badly armed— there were only twenty-five guns for the five hundred soldiers in a battalion from Drôme—and not used to living under military discipline, these volunteers encountered defeat after defeat at the beginning of hostilities. On August 19 the Prussians of Brunswick's army entered Lorraine; on September 2 they took Verdun-sur-Meuse. The road to Paris lay open before them. Danton, who proclaimed, "Everything belongs to the country when the country is in danger," galvanized the enthusiasm of the Parisians.

To the strains of "La Marseillaise," the "army of cobblers and tailors" reached the plains of Champagne. On September 20 the Prussian army of thirty-four thousand men met the army of fifty thousand improvised soldiers at Valmy. From a knoll at Valmy, General Kellermann encouraged his troops with a "Vive la nation!" The battalions threw themselves on the paralyzed Prussians. The latter, their ranks already thinned by an epidemic of dysentery, fell back. The Revolution was saved; the war of revolutionary propaganda and of con-

Before the representative of the Republic, a young sansculotte signs up as two national guardsmen look on. Some of these volunteers would serve under the tricolor flags of the Revolution, then of the Empire, until 1815!

Since June 5, 1793, when the Montgolfier brothers flew their first hot-air balloon, experiments in flight had multiplied. On October 15 of the same year, Jean-François Pilâtre de Rosier, before Louis XVI and the court, rose into the air in a tethered balloon. Accompanied by the Marquis d'Arlandes on November 21, he flew over Paris without his balloon being attached to the ground. Humans had finally realized the dream of Icarus. The battle of Fleurus was the first occasion on which the military utilized the balloon. The tethered balloon, although a remarkable observation post, had one drawback: since it was filled with hydrogen, there was a risk of explosion from the smallest spark.

quest had begun. The next day the Republic was proclaimed. On November 6, General Dumouriez threw the dense mass of the "barefoot army" against the Austrian army and won the battle at Jemappes. The republican army then conquered Belgium, which was then an Austrian possession. But soon dissension split the victorious army ranks. The army of the line—in white uniforms—detested the volunteers in their blue jackets, who were nicknamed *bleuets* (blue flowers) or *faiences bleues* ("blue crocks"). Fights and duels were frequent. To stop the conflicts that threatened to destroy the army's unity, some revolutionaries proposed amalgamation: one line battalion would join with two volunteer battalions and a company of artillery.

As the months passed, the war spread and all of Europe—England, Holland, Sardinia, Spain—united against France. To fight back, the Convention decided on February 23, 1793, to recruit 300,000 men. When the recruiting went badly, the Convention sent deputies called "representatives on mission" to the departments. On August 23 a mass levy had to be declared. Lack of enthusiasm was obvious. Many soldiers deserted. In addition, not only was the republican army ill-equipped, it was often at the mercy of unscrupulous suppliers. For instance, in the army of the North, the sabers of six hundred hussars, or cavalry soldiers, bent like lead! From summer to autumn 1793, new defeats accumulated. To ease the shortage of arms, the Convention requisitioned all workers in metal, from the blacksmith to the goldsmith. Forges were installed everywhere. There were 250 of them in Paris alone. To acquire enough bronze a decree allowed the confiscation of all church bells. The government also urged citizens to collect saltpeter to make gunpowder. Public courses on the "tyrannicidal powder" were held. People had to clean out their cellars, stables, storerooms, and winepresses. . . .

At the end of the year 1793, new victories could at last be celebrated at Hondschoote and Wattignies, and finally at Fleurus on June 26, 1794, where a tethered balloon was used for observation by the French General Staff. The soldiers of the Republic had given victorious meaning to their motto: "Conquer or die."

The Death of the King

On September 21, 1792, as Paris learned with relief of the victory at Valmy, the 745 deputies of the Convention met for the first time and declared the end of the monarchy. But as they agreed to make France a republic, they differed on the fate of the king. Robespierre and Louis Antoine Léon de Saint-Just believed that Louis XVI should be put to death without a trial: "Louis has been dethroned because he called on the armies of the tyrants, his confreres, to punish the people. The victory of August 10 has shown that he alone was the rebel." But most of the Convention members wanted to have a trial, and after the secret correspondence of Louis XVI was discovered in an iron cupboard at the Tuileries, revealing overwhelming proof of his treachery, they were even further determined that he should be tried.

On December 21, "Louis Capet, until now king of France," appeared before the Convention, which had been set up as a tribunal. In spite of his defenders, who pleaded that the person of the king could not be tried, the tribunal proceeded toward a sentence of death.

The moderate deputies, believing that the death of the king would lead to war once again and give the sansculottes a chance to gain more power, did all they could to save Louis XVI. They asked that the verdict be submitted for the approval of the people, but the maneuver failed.

On January 18 the deputies, one by one as their names were called, recognized the guilt of the king by a crushing majority. Still, only 361 of the 721 who took part in the vote pronounced a sentence of immediate death.

Condemning the king was not easy. Even for his fiercest adversaries he remained, in spite of everything, a sort of sacred personage. Robespierre declared later that he felt his "heart reel, in the presence of the humiliated and guilty monarch."

On January 20, at two o'clock in the morning, the king learned of the deputies' decision. He asked to see his family and to receive a nonjurist priest to hear his confession. At nine o'clock, Marie Antoinette and her two children entered his cell. "There were tears and sobs, then a fairly calm conversation." A short while later the king made his confession, heard mass, and took communion. In the evening, after having said goodbye to his family, the king had supper. His valet, Cléry, related: "With a good appetite he ate two chicken wings and a few vegetables, drank two glasses of water and wine, and for dessert took a little sponge cake and some Malaga wine." As soon as he went to bed, he slept deeply.

Awakened at five o'clock, he attended his last mass. He had to let the executioner shave the hair covering his neck. At half past eight he left the Temple prison. Windows and doors had been shut all along the route taken by his carriage. Eighty thousand armed guards guaranteed order. At ten o'clock, on the Place de la Révolution (the former Place Louis XV), the sinister silhouette of the guillotine awaited. The king, in shirtsleeves, his hands bound behind his back, mounted the steps of the scaffold.

His face reddened with emotion, the king tried to go forward and speak, but several voices shouted for the executioners to do their duty. The drums rolled. As the executioners were strapping him down and before the plank shook under the horrible machine, the king addressed the crowd, who did not hear him: "I die innocent, I forgive my enemies. May my blood be useful to France, may it appease the anger of God." At ten-twenty in the morning, the knife fell.

As the headsman brandished the king's head, cries of "Vive la République" arose. But a France governed by regicides no longer had anything but enemies in Europe. "Now we are really cut off. We have burned our bridges behind us," wrote the deputy Le Bas. By cutting off the head of its king, the Revolution had untied the last knot binding the country to its past.

Robespierre and the Pain of Death . . .

"Every ferocious horde of despotism is preparing, in the name of Louis XVI, to tear apart once more the heart of our country. Louis still fights us from the depths of his dungeon. . . .

"As far as I am concerned, I abhor the death penalty . . . and I have neither love nor hate for Louis; I hate only his heinous crimes. . . . I pronounce this fatal truth regretfully—but Louis must die so that the country may live. . . .

I demand that the National Convention declare him, from this moment, a traitor to the French nation, a criminal before humanity."

From a speech of December 3, 1792

The War
in the Vendée

On March 3, 1793, a fairly large crowd had formed at Cholet to oppose the recruitment of soldiers as decreed by the Convention. To cries of "No drawing!" (drawing by lots) and "Down with the militia!" the youth of the Vendée department rose in rebellion. At two o'clock in the morning, the citizen who was second-in-command in the National Guard tried to calm the crowd down. He was handled roughly. Someone, mad with rage, snatched his saber and wounded him in the head.

Ten days later, toward the end of the afternoon, a crowd of peasants and tradespeople, armed with guns, pitchforks, and sickles, and all wearing white cockades, presented themselves at the little town of St.-Pierre crying, "Vive le roi! Long live our good priests! We want them back and we want the old regime! We are going to cut the patriots' throats." The entire mob threw itself on the national guardsmen, killing some of them, and dispersing the rest. The inhabitants of the rebellious parishes asked for help from the local nobles, knowing they were trained in warfare. In one place, Monsieur de Sapineau had to be persuaded to take command; in another it was Bonchamp, Henri de la Roche-Jacquelein, and d'Elbée; in still another, Charrette was named. They took savage revenge on the bourgeoisie of the cities, on the "gentlemen" who were buying up the national property on a grand scale, and on mayors who had been excused from military service. At Machecoul, peasant anger resulted in 175 victims having their throats cut in one day. One horror brought on another. At Savenay a republican general, Westerman, wrote: "We shot two thousand brigands. It's called 'sending them to the field hospital.' We also put them in boats that were then sunk. That's called 'sending them to the water castle.' "

South of the Loire, for seven months, the royal Catholic army of the "Whites" (Royalists) waged a victorious war against the "Blues" (Republicans).

At the beginning of the uprising, the Blues—who were mostly young recruits

with little training—lay down at the moment of attack if they did not flee, unnerved by the fire of the Vendéans.

In the spring and summer of 1793, the Whites—whose number varied between thirty thousand and seventy thousand men, depending on the date—seized several cities, including Angers on June 20. But they failed to take Nantes, where they lost their best general, Jacques Cathelineau, who had been nicknamed the Saint of Anjou. The army of the Vendéans was not suited for classical warfare with pitched battles and sieges of strongholds. What it excelled in was guerrilla warfare. And the wooded terrain of Vendée, with its labyrinths of quickset hedges and winding paths, lent itself marvelously to this kind of warfare.

Constantly harassed and living with fear in the pit of their stomachs, the republican troops fired wildly whenever they were attacked, whereas the Whites took time to aim at their targets. The Blues lost five men for every one that the Whites lost! After carrying out their ambushes, the Whites withdrew into their villages and resumed the life of inoffensive peasants.

At all times the insurgents were kept informed of the republican army positions. The millers put their windmills at the service of the insurrection. If the windmills were turning and the winds were carrying their sails, then there was no danger; if the windmills had stopped, the Blues were in sight; if the sails were off, it was a sign that the enemy was there in strength. In spite of these tricks, however, the republicans, by weight of their numbers, carried off victory after victory in the autumn of 1793. The royalist army waited in vain for help from the British. The time had come for the Whites to retreat, and they finished doing so on December 23 in the marshes of Savenay. Eighty thousand men, women, and children, hunted by the republicans, left nearly ten thousand dead behind them.

The war was truly ended. The Whites had suffered nearly 100,000 deaths. Although the Vendéans continued to fight until 1800, they no longer presented the mortal danger that they had presented for the Revolution during the year 1793.

The Infernal Columns

From January to May 1794, twelve republican columns, nicknamed the infernal columns, were to save the Vendée with fire and bloodshed. Whole villages were put to the sword. At Petit Luc, 563 people were massacred with bayonets or burned alive; 110 of them were children less than seven years old.

"I have burned and set ablaze all the houses and cut the throats of all the inhabitants of Palluau. I estimate that since January I have destroyed three thousand men, two thousand of whom were taken without arms," wrote General Duquesnoy coldly.

The Girondists and the Montagnards

Ever since it first met, in September 1792, the Convention had been dominated by the Girondists, who with the support of moderate deputies formed a group called the Plain which controlled the government.

In the Assembly as well as at the Jacobin Club, the Girondists advocated a policy of economic freedom. At the same time they denounced, through the journalist Brissot de Warville, a brilliant orator, "all those who would equalize everything—property, wealth, the price of goods, even talent, knowledge, and the virtues, because they have none of these." The Girondists met in the salon of Madame Roland, an intelligent, brilliant, and courageous woman that all of Paris said told her husband, one of the king's ministers in 1792, what policies he was to follow. In this salon's informal gatherings the Jacobins debated, along with the philosopher Condorcet, the measures that they proposed to the Convention and later voted on.

The adversaries of the Girondists were the Montagnards, or members of the party of *La montagne* ("the mountain"), so called because they occupied the highest tiers of seats in the Assembly. The leaders of the Montagnards, Robespierre, Danton, Jean-Paul Marat, were not much different from the leaders of the Girondists. They were all members of the bourgeoisie or of minor nobility without large fortunes, and their policies were not very different. What really made them opponents was the struggle for power. This power was controlled by the Girondists in the autumn of 1792, but the uprising in Vendée, the military defeats, and the anger of the people of Paris forced the Girondists to relinquish their power by the spring of 1793.

Paris had elected a majority of the Montagnards, but the sansculottes preferred to recognize as their representatives Jacques-René Hébert and Pierre-Gaspard Chaumette, leaders of the Insurrectional Commune that was formed on August 10, 1792, which continued to occupy the town hall. The *sectionnaires,* or national guardsmen of the populist quarters, were demanding violent measures against the émigrés and the rich landowners, whom the guardsmen accused of being responsible for the rise in prices.

At the Convention the Montagnards backed the demands of the sansculottes to get rid of the Girondists. Marat wanted to remove from office all deputies who had not voted for the immediate death of the king in January 1793. The Girondists had Marat tried by the Revolutionary Tribunal, accusing him of attempting to install a dictatorship. But the trial favored Marat. Known as the "Friend of the People," Marat was acquitted, crowned with oak leaves, and carried in triumph through the streets of the capital.

In spite of this setback, the Girondists, who wanted to suppress the Insurrectional Commune, had Hébert arrested. To the sansculottes, who came to demand that he be freed, the Girondist Isnard retorted: "If the Convention were to be interfered with, Paris would be destroyed. Paris must be reduced to one eighty-third part of its (governing) influence."

Just as the takeover of the Tuileries palace on August 10, 1792, had been a response to the Brunswick Manifesto (the proclamation of a Prussian general who supported King Louis XVI that he would destroy Paris), so now Robespierre organized a plot in reply to the Girondist menace; the plot was to take place on June 2, 1793.

During the night of May 29, the delegates from thirty-three of the forty-eight Parisian districts created a secret insurrectional committee. A sansculotte named François Hanriot was appointed head of the National Guard. On May 31 the rebels invaded the Convention and demanded the arrest of the Girondist leaders. The rebels also wanted to buy bread at three sous a pound (although it cost five sous), and they wanted the setting up of an army of sansculottes who would have the right to vote reserved solely for them. But the rebels gained nothing. On Sunday, June 2, Hanriot posted eighty thousand men around the Convention and threatened: "If within the hour the Assembly has not delivered up the Girondists, I will destroy it with my cannons." Inside the Hall,

Georges Couthon, a deputy from the Montagnards, expressed his pleasure at this demand. Vergniaud, a Girondist, shouted: "Give Couthon a glass of blood; he is thirsty!" The Convention gave in to the sansculottes and decreed the arrest of the Girondists, many of whom, however, succeeded in escaping. The Montagnards took power, thanks to the sansculottes, their turbulent allies for a day.

The provinces, however, remained faithful to the Girondists. In July 1793 more than half the departments were in rebellion against Paris, where the revolutionary government was exercising a veritable dictatorship.

A Meeting at the Jacobin Club

In May 1793, Robespierre was relying on the Jacobins of Paris to attack the Girondists. In his elegant striped outfit, well-groomed as always, his wig and face powdered, he is making accusations against his adversaries, who are trying to cut him short. In front of him are seated Saint-Just and Danton, Montagnards like himself. They are prepared to support him, should the need arise.

The Revolutionary Government

Confronted with the dangers looming before it both at home and on the nation's frontiers, the Convention, using exceptional methods, had to enact new policies speedily.

In March 1973 a new decree ordered that a committee called the Committee of Surveillance be set up in each community. Each committee was elected by all the men of the village and met three times a week. Its president was changed every two weeks. These committees had the task of issuing to travelers who passed through the community certificates of good citizenship without which they would become suspect and of making up lists of émigrés and their families who should appear before the Revolutionary Tribunal. The committees also made certain that no one was selling wheat or flour at a price higher than the maximum fixed by the Convention on May 4, 1793, and listed the fortunes of the wealthy, who had to underwrite a forced loan of one billion francs.

The Committee of Public Safety, created by the Convention on April 6, directed and controlled the entire policy of the Revolution. After their victory over the Girondists, the Montagnards strengthened their position during the summer of 1793. With his strong personality, Robespierre dominated the government. He was assisted by Saint-Just and by Couthon, who took over direction of the political police. To the moderate Lazare-Nicoles Margue-

This former aristocrat, who had emigrated in 1789 and returned to France to try to recover his possessions, has run out of luck. He betrayed himself hardly an hour earlier by using vous *instead of the more familiar* tu *when talking to fellow citizens and by addressing the innkeeper where he was lodging incognito as "Madame" instead of "Citizeness."*

Having been denounced immediately, he is being arrested by two members of the Comité de Surveillance *("Committee of Surveillance"), and a national guardsman lends a helping hand.*

rite Carnot was left the heavy burden of directing the war. Jean-Nicolas Billaud-Varenne and Jean-Marie Collot d'Herbois dispatched representatives on mission into the departments to reestablish republican order, by force if necessary.

The General Security Committee paid closer attention to suspects, too. Its members, all Montagnards, often traveled into the provinces to meet with the presidents of each Committee of Surveillance. They fired up the zeal of certain presidents who had been allowing prisoners to live with their families and their furniture in their cells, sometimes permitting the prisoners to "walk freely outside the prison"!

The Stillborn Constitution

Since August 10, 1792, France had been without a constitution. At the Convention the deputies worked to draft a text; they published a new declaration of the rights of man, which stated that "the aim of society is the common happiness." To those rights already acknowledged in 1789, the Declaration added the right to work, to help in need, to education, and even to insurrection!

The Constitution also gave the people a greater political role. They would henceforth be consulted by means of referendums that would allow them to vote for or against laws. On August 10, 1793, the new Constitution was adopted by 1.7 million electors. Only seventeen thousand voted against it, but more than four million Frenchmen did not take part in the polling. Two months later the Convention decided not to initiate the Constitution as long as the war lasted.

Under a bust of Marat, the Martyr of the Revolution, and under the Declaration of the Rights of Man and of the Citizen, members of one Committee of Surveillance are examining a traveler's papers before making out his certificate of good citizenship.

According to their mood at the moment, the members will let him have the certificate immediately, tell him to come back for further questioning, or, sometimes, provide him with the precious document only in exchange for a small fee that they will use to drink to the Republic's health.

Lyons No Longer Exists

In 1792, Lyons, like Paris, experienced its September massacres. The sansculottes chose a Jacobin, Chalier, as their leader and turned to insurrection. They destroyed all symbols of royalty on buildings and solemnly burned the portraits of the city's former mayor. The unruly crowd massacred some military officers and took off for the prisons, cutting the throats of the detainees there, whose heads, stuck on the ends of their pikes, became trophies of these macabre days. In groups, impoverished citizens paid visits to the grocers, fixed the prices of goods themselves, and ransacked the shops, emptying them of all their stock.

In February 1793, the deputies of the Montagnards, who had seized the town hall, used Chalier as a spokesman and proposed a scheme that contained everything guaranteed to please the sansculottes: "The great day of vengeance has arrived; the city must be purged. Five hundred heads deserve the same fate as that of the tyrant [Louis XVI]. The capitalists, the rich, and the dilettantes must be taxed." Openly threatened with death, the Girondists of Lyons took up arms. On May 29 they besieged the town hall, where Chalier and the Montagnards, defended by eighteen hundred sansculottes and national guardsmen, managed to push back the first attacks. But soon the Girondist cannon put an end to the resistance. Chalier surrendered and was immediately imprisoned.

When the Girondists of Lyons learned that in Paris the takeover of June 2 had put the Montagnards in power, they decided to no longer obey the decrees of the Convention and raised a battalion of volunteers to march on the capital. Chalier, who had dreamed of "washing my hands in the blood of the members of the department," was guillotined on July 27. The city was put in a state of siege; the royalists, who believed their hour had come, joined with the Girondists and made one of their own, the Count de Précy, head of the eight thousand defenders of the city.

On August 8, General Kellermann, the hero of Valmy and the commander of the army of the Alps, had the city surrounded. A month later the people of Lyons had no food and had to take hay from their horses to make bread! The representatives on mission, dispatched to the scene by the Committee of Public Safety, repeatedly told the peasants in the surrounding countryside that the insurgents were trying to reinstate the old regime and bring devastation and death to the area.

At the beginning of October, Kellermann's cannons let out a hail of shot on the left bank of the Rhone. As a result the Perrache district was ravaged by a gigantic fire, fanned by a high wind. On October 9, Précy had to evacuate the city with the remainder of his troops. Lyons capitulated and was delivered helpless to the terrible vengeance of the Montagnards.

At the Committee of Public Safety, Bertrand Barère declared: "Lyons made the blood of patriots run. It should be buried under its ruins. What should be spared? The homes of the indigent and the factories. But all the rest must be plowed under. Lyons made war with liberty. Lyons no longer exists; you will call it the emancipated city."

Repression descended on the city. After October 12, Joseph Fouché, the representative on mission, set the tone: "Anything is permitted to those who are acting as revolutionaries!" Thousands of people were crowded into prisons. Before being tried, they had to suffer the mockery of their jailers: "You, you'll have your head put through the cattrap; you, you'll put yours through the red window. . . ."

The judges, dressed in military uniform, did not even bother to pronounce sentences. At the end of the interrogation, if the judges touched the axe, it meant the guillotine; if they put their hands to their brows, it meant the prisoner would be shot; if they stretched their hands out on the table—and they did so rarely—it meant acquittal. At the rate of seven verdicts every ten minutes, they condemned two thousand people in this way.

Those about to be shot were bound two by two, led between two trenches, and mowed down by cannon fire. They were then finished off by saber thrusts from soldiers.

Beribboned and decked out in the tricolor, the représentant en mission ("representative on mission") observes the last moments of the Lyonnais uprising. Entrusted with seeing that the orders of the Convention and the Committee of Public Safety are carried out, the representative commands enormous power. Simply by writing a letter he can deprive a general of his command and have him tried by the Revolutionary Tribunal. Fouché, who directed the suppression of Lyons, behaved like a tyrant.

The Revolutionary Tribunal

Officially instituted on March 10, 1793, the Revolutionary Tribunal was set up to try crimes against the Republic. Adhering to the rules that had been in force since the Constituent Assembly, it sat in the Palace of Justice in Paris. The public prosecutor, Antoine-Quentin Fouquier-Tinville, was in charge of prosecuting each crime. The judges heard witnesses in the presence of juries who decided the guilt or innocence of the accused. Finally the judges meted out punishments according to the law. The sentences could not be appealed, and the trials were public.

From March to September 1793, the Revolutionary Tribunal tried 260 of the accused and condemned only 66 to death. But when the Reign of Terror started, the Convention, fearing that the sansculottes would themselves impose "revolutionary justice," passed exceptional laws that threw all suspects named by the vigilance committees into prison. Swamped by the number of trials, Fouquier-Tinville complained that he could no longer carry out his task. During the trial of the Girondists, in October 1793, he declared: "For five days we have been held up by the legal procedures. The trial will be interminable if the Convention does not suppress all these formalities."

In the name of the sansculottes, Hébert condemned this "culpable slowness" before the Jacobins and in the pages of his newspaper. A decree provided that after three days of debate and with the consent of the jury, the judge could stop the hear-

ing and pronounce the sentence immediately, be it prison, deportation, the guillotine, or acquittal. The Revolutionary Tribunal, no longer respecting the rights of the defense, ceased to render justice and became a killing machine in the hands of the revolutionary government.

In the spring of 1794, when there were no longer any threats to the Republic, Robespierre and his friends had the law of 22 *Prairial* year II (June 10, 1794) voted on by the Assembly. (*Prairial* was the ninth month, May–June, of the republican calendar). The accused were now interrogated the first time at a hearing. They no longer had the right to be defended by a lawyer. If the president of the Tribunal thought there was sufficient proof against the accused, no witnesses were called. The Revolutionary Tribunal could now pronounce only one sentence—death.

The Tribunal often tried cases that were arranged. For example, the Committee of General Security invented a prison conspiracy. Fouquier-Tinville received daily reports on the behavior of the prisoners. He sometimes drew up bills of indictment based on imaginary crimes. The clerks prepared death sentences in advance, with only the name remaining to be inserted.

When one of the accused tried to plead innocence, the judges would cut the person short and threaten to exclude the culprit from the proceedings. "You knew the Lévi women who were guillotined?" Alexander Davy de la Pailleterie, known as Dumas, vice president of the Tribunal, was interrogating. The elderly Maréchale de Noailles replied: "Citizen, we did pay them a visit but . . ." "Silence!" howled Dumas. "You have heard, citizen jurymen, she knew the Lévi women, therefore. . . ." Thus, she would mount the scaffold.

The deputies of the Convention, who had created the Tribunal, watched as little by little their handiwork got out of control. Many of them wondered when their turn to appear before their creation would come. Between June and July 1794, the Tribunal sent 1,376 victims to the guillotine, whereas they condemned 1,271 between March 1793 and April 1794. Among the victims were not only aristocrats but also bourgeoisie, sansculottes, and peasants. The Revolution was devouring its own children!

A Session of the Revolutionary Tribunal

From the witness box a sansculotte is staring at the accused, who are surrounded by the National Guard. On his right the members of the jury are listening inattentively. The judges are waiting for the public prosecutor to finish his indictment before allowing the accused, or their lawyers, if they have any, to speak. The courtroom is crowded with the public. For some women these sessions have become an entertainment. They spend their days here, jostling each other early in the morning at the entrance to the palace to be sure of having a place in the front row. Busy with their knitting, which they never lay down except during the most intense moments of the trial, these tricoteuses *("knitters"), all fervent patriots, do not hesitate to harangue the judges and the jury when they consider them too lenient with the accused for whom they demand a more expeditious procedure. They were delighted with the decree of 22 Prairial year II!*

The Reign of Terror

On September 5, 1793, "the Terror was put on the agenda." Under ever-increasing pressure from the sansculottes, the Convention passed the Law of Suspects. To be imprisoned were "those who have shown themselves to be partisans of tyranny or federalism and enemies of liberty."

On October 16 the Revolutionary Tribunal had the former queen, Marie Antoinette, executed. A few days later, twenty-two Girondist deputies and Madame Roland mounted the scaffold in their turn, just before Louis XV's former favorite, Madame du Barry.

At Nantes the repression was even more brutal than at Lyons. Jean-Baptiste Carrier, the representative on mission, had six thousand people put to death there. Most of them, chained on boats that were then sunk, drowned in the Loire, which was then christened the "national bathtub" by the sansculottes.

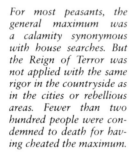

For most peasants, the general maximum was a calamity synonymous with house searches. But the Reign of Terror was not applied with the same rigor in the countryside as in the cities or rebellious areas. Fewer than two hundred people were condemned to death for having cheated the maximum.

But the people demanded even more blood. Threatened with famine, they made their accusations by means of Hébert's pen: "Traders have no country. They have seized all goods and all supplies so as to resell them for huge prices." The Convention yielded again and granted the "general maximum," a ruling that fixed the price of food, salaries, and profits.

The cure, however, was worse than the disease. Merchants and peasants hid their goods in the depths of their cellars. The revolutionary committees had to organize house searches, which often proved useless. The government threatened death to all those found to be holding large sums in gold. The wealthy rushed to change their money into assignats, or promissory notes, thus regaining some of their value. The general maximum eventually failed. It was applied only where the sansculottes were numerous enough and determined enough to have it obeyed.

At the Committee of Public Safety, Robespierre and his friends, supporters of economic freedom, were determined to rid themselves of the most troublesome of the sansculotte leaders. They began in Septem-

Madame Roland
As the crowd howled "Death!" she remained calm and collected, replying, "I am going!"

Madame du Barry
"When she got to the scaffold, she had to be tied forcibly to the fatal plank. Her last words were, 'Mercy! Mercy, Monsieur executioner! Just another minute, Monsieur executioner! Just . . .' And she was silenced!"

Marie Antoinette
Arriving in front of the scaffold, she stepped on the executioner's foot and said to him, "Excuse me!"

One aristocrat casually read a book in the cart that was taking him to the guillotine. When his turn came to climb the steps of the scaffold, he sighed, turned down the corner of the page he was reading, and shut the book, as if he was sure of being able to resume his reading in the hereafter.

ber 1793 by having Jacques Roux, a former priest who directed the extremist group of the *Enragés* ("Enraged Ones") arrested. In December, and with Danton's help, Robespierre attacked Hébert and his supporters, the *Exagérés* ("Exaggerated Ones"), who were organizing "dechristianization." Robespierre said, "He who wishes to abolish Christianity is just as fanatical as he who says mass."

In his newspaper *Le Père Duchesne*, Hébert replied by advocating an acceleration of the Terror: "The butchers who treat the sansculottes like dogs and give them only bones to gnaw are playing with fire [should be guillotined]."

During the night of 23 to 24 *Ventôse* (March 13 to 14), 1794, Hébert and his friends were arrested. After ten days of a faked trial, they were condemned and executed.

Life in the Prisons

After July 1793, the fifteen prisons of Paris were always full. At Bicêtre the number of detainees was two hundred in July and six hundred in another three months. At the Force, the number of suspects and counterrevolutionaries went from 450 to more than a thousand. During the same period the complement of the Conciergerie, the antechamber of the guillotine, was swollen by almost three hundred extra prisoners.

The former Collège du Plessis had been converted into a prison. In it were crammed not only "victims of every age" that the Conciergerie could no longer take but also those who had been accused in the provinces. So many arrived during the autumn of 1793 that the walls of the College of Louis-le-Grand that were next to the cells had to be broken through to accommodate the newcomers.

The women, shut up in attics that were stifling in summer and freezing in winter, were allowed out for one hour each day. Their children, who had been shut up with them, had no food but the prisoners' bread and water, for often "their mothers can only procure a few supplies that a greedy caterer sells dearly."

The meals in general were vile. In the Luxembourg prison, the eight hundred to one thousand prisoners were placed at large wooden tables. A caterer served a foul soup for 50 sols, a dish of "dry vegetables, full of hair, mud, and worms" and some bits of spoiled pork mixed with fermented cabbage. The whole mess was washed down with a potion that he dared to call wine. The prison director did not concern himself with quality; he was content to shrug his shoulders and pocket the gratuity provided by the caterer.

In April 1794 the regimen in the prisons was made more severe. The prisoners, deprived of their personal belongings, including their knives and forks, had to "tear at the meat with their fingers."

Corruption reigned throughout. Jailers rented beds in the "first-class rooms" at

exorbitant prices to the wealthiest prisoners, and the "straw buyers" had to lie on litters of straw not fit for use in a stable. At Ste.-Pélagie the keeper of the keys, "in a raucous voice with an undertone of menace," asked each new arrival: "Do you have any bells?" (money). If the answer was yes, a jug of water and a basin were handed out. If it was no, the reply was, "Well, so much the worse for you, but you don't get anything with nothing."

Under such conditions, epidemics spread. The sick were crowded two to a pallet and received the usual single allotment of tea no matter what condition they were in.

Every day, at the hour when the gates were closed, the roll call was held. "Imagine to yourself three or four turnkeys, all drunk and with half a dozen pointer dogs, holding in their hands incorrect lists that they cannot read. They shout a name; no one recognizes himself or herself. The turnkeys swear, storm, and threaten; then they try again. People explain and help them. At last an understanding is reached."

The harshness of life in prison inspired mutual help and solidarity. Aristocrats, magistrates, priests, and bankers banded with peasants and even sansculottes. In their common anguish, everyone forgot any bad feelings. At the Lazare prison the rich got together to give the poorest enough money to allow them to survive in decency. At the Conciergerie, every morning the aristocratic ladies washed and dried their single garment. At the Madelonnettes the prisoners amused themselves by playing music after a fashion. Elsewhere, ball games, songs, poems, and, sometimes, dances filled up the days that for some prisoners would be their last.

When the officer from the Revolutionary Tribunal came to fetch "the thirty or forty winners of the lottery of Saint Guillotine," the condemned left their companions in misfortune, saying, "Let our people know that we died with courage."

A Village at the Time of the Revolution

On September 24, 1792, French armies pushed back the armies belonging to the king of Sardinia and entered Savoy, then a Sardinian province. On October 21, the National Assembly of the Allobroges (a Celtic people who had lived in the area since Roman times) met at Chambéry. This Assembly decided to abolish the monarchy, tithes, and all privileges and feudal rights, and called for the union of Savoy with France. On November 27, 1792, Savoy became Mont-Blanc, the eighty-fourth department of the Republic.

The village of Viry (today, part of Upper Savoy) called several meetings of its municipal council every week during the period 1793 to 1795. The secretary took careful notes of the proceedings. Thanks to these invaluable archives, we are able to see how the inhabitants of Viry lived through the Revolution.

February 7, 1793: "A vote was taken to nominate a mayor, and its result gave all the votes to citizen Joseph-Marie Viry, who was proclaimed mayor to the unanimous applause of the Assembly." (Joseph-Marie Viry, a nobleman who belonged to the council before the Revolution, remained mayor during most of its course.)

February 23, 1793: "The council, declaring that municipal officers, to uphold the dignity of their offices, should be decorated by the tricolor scarf . . . has decided to take the amount of this expense out of the communal funds."

March 18, 1793: "The community having nationalized the property of the clergy, the council decrees that all former ecclesiastical property will be put up for public auction on the twenty-sixth current."

May 16, 1793: "The council invites the citizen-mayor to be good enough to assume the functions of public officer and to record the births and deaths of the citizens as well as to preside at marriages."

July 14, 1793: "In reply to a questionnaire sent by the administration of the district of Carouge, the council is sending on information about the village of Viry. The population consists of 990 inhabitants, including forty-two children born in 1792, and nineteen born in the first six months of this year. The number of marriages was six in 1792 and eleven this year. The number of deaths was twenty-two in 1792 and twelve so far this year."

September 8, 1793: "The council certifies that none of the ex-nobles domiciled in the community has emigrated, and they are at present living in their old homes. As to the former nuns, only one is known. She resides at Humilly, at the home of citizen Christopher Chevilly. . . ."

October 3, 1793: "The council, considering that the two bells in its possession are absolutely necessary to it, one in the service of the community and the other, much smaller one, to sound the strokes of the clock situated in the belfry . . . suspends, for clocks, the carrying out of the decree of the National Convention of last July 23."

8 *Frimaire* year II (November 28, 1793) [*Frimaire* was the third month, November–December, of the republican calendar.] (The Revolutionary calendar was officially adopted on October 24, 1793):"The council, in consideration of the maximum fixed . . . for the price of wine, decrees that a bottle of wine will be sold by innkeepers, tavernkeepers, and others, at six sous for red wine and seven sous for white wine. . . ."

26 *Ventôse,* year II (March 16, 1794): "By demand of the national agent, citizen Albert Rouge, carpenter, is appointed to inspect the work carried out by citizen Mouthon to deface the former belfry. Also, the council is taking bids for the contract to close up the openings of said belfry . . . and for the removal of the holy water basins and baptismal fonts that are still standing in the former church."

12 *Germinal* year II (April 1, 1794): "On the report by councilor Claude Cusin that three young men of the community did not present themselves with the others at Carouge yesterday for the military draft, the council, profoundly affected by the cowardice of these young men, decrees that the National Guard will be ordered to put them under arrest."

5 _Floréal_ year II (April 24, 1794): The council protests the arrest of its mayor, Joseph-Marie Viry, imprisoned because he is a noble. "The municipality has been struck by paralysis from the moment that citizen Viry, whose private and political life honors the man and the citizen—he, the warmest defender of liberty; he, who has constantly identified himself with the success of the people's cause; he, who has never deviated from a career of patriotism; he, who has bent all his efforts to make the revolutionary government work, to have the laws honored and virtue loved; he, who indeed was the constitutional Hercules of this canton . . . Yes, from the moment this virtuous republican was removed from his post as mayor. . . ." (The mayor was freed after 9 _Thermidor_ year II.)

14 _Prairial_ year II (June 13, 1794): "The council, having heard the reading of a decree for the district . . . declaring that a workshop for making saltpeter will be established in Viry, announces that the former vicarage will be set apart for this use."

1 _Ventôse_ year III (February 19, 1795): "The Mestrallet couple presented themselves at the meeting and showed the teaching certificates that the members of the district selection committee for public education had given them."

13 _Brumaire_ year IV (November 3, 1795): "The citizen-mayor . . . pronounced the dissolution of the council of Viry." (This was because the new Constitution created the Directory, [a complete change of government in France].)

"Here we are honored by the title of citizen."

"*The practices and formulas of politeness were conceived in fear and servitude; it is a superstition that must be swept away by the winds of liberty and equality.*" So wrote the journalist Carra in 1789. Some time later, the sansculottes demanded that the "aristocratic monsieur and madame" be suppressed and replaced by the words citizen and citizeness. On the doors of the popular clubs, on the walls of government offices, the phrase "Here we are honored by the title of citizen" soon flourished.

In the spring of 1793, the theaters are crowded. "The Benevolent Churl" is playing. On the stage, two actors are playing a game of chess. One of them raises his arm in the sign of victory. Everyone expects the ritual "Check the king," but it is "Check the tyrant" that is heard. Thunderous applause greets this reply.

All during the Revolution, the revolutionary assemblies and the French people pledged themselves to transforming their daily life, even in its smallest details. They wanted to create a new fraternity so as to prevent the return of the aristocratic past. After 1790, titles of nobility were forbidden. Some citizens became indignant that "former seigneurs had the conceit to give their family names to parishes." From then on, communities would be renamed. Under the Convention, this movement spread—names of saints and châteaus were systematically changed. In September 1794, Bourg-la-Reine (Hauts-de-Seine) became Bourg-l'Egalité ("Equality"), Brie-Compte-Robert (Seine et Marne) became Brie-Libre ("Free"), St.-Loup-de-la-Salle (Saône-et-Loire) was transformed into Arbre-Vert ("Green Tree"), and St.-Germain-en Laye (Yvelines) into Montagne-Bon-Air ("Good Air Mountain"). Other communities used the names of great men of the past, of Greek or Roman antiquity. Montfort-l'Amaury (Yvelines) became Montfort-le-Brutus. Communities called themselves Marathon or even Hercules. St.-Tropez was metamorphosed into Heracles (Hercules in Greek). The symbols of the sansculottes were also honored. In the Ardennes, Han-les-Moines traded its name for Han-les-Sans-culottes! Croix ("Cross")-Chapeau (Charente-Maritime) became Pique ("Pike")-Chapeau, St.-Bonnet-Elvert (Corrèze) became Liberté-Bonnet-Rouge. Montmartre became Mont-Marat, Villedieu in Charente-Maritime did not hesitate to rechristen itself with the name of the famous song "La Carmagnole." On the other hand, the cities and departments that had opposed the Convention of the Montagnards were punished—Marseilles, for instance, was called Nameless by Barras and Frénom, and the Vendée lost its identity, to become "Département Vengé," or "Avenged Department."

The Convention members Philippe Fabre d'Églantine and Charles Romme were also committed to changing the calendar. The year was twelve months of thirty days (plus five complementary days), and it began at the autumnal equinox, corresponding to the day of the proclamation of the Republic, September 22, 1792. Thus, September 1793 began Year II of the new era. Each month was divided into decades of ten days called primidi, duodi, and so on. For the names of saints, Fabre d'Églantine substituted names of trees, grains, roots, and flowers, and each décadi, replacing Sunday, was given a name that corresponded to an agricultural instrument. The names of the months were changed, too. For autumn, Vendémiaire (for the vendanges, or grape harvests) represented September—October; Brumaire (for the brumes, or mists), October—November; Frimaire (for the frosts), November—December. For winter the names were Nivose (snow), Pluviose (rain), and Ventose (wind), for the spring, Germinal (seed-time), Floreal (blossom), Prairial (meadow). Finally, for summer the names were Messidor (harvest), Thermidor (heat), and Fructidor (fruits). In 1806, the republican calendar disappeared in favor of the traditional calendar, which is still used.

The patriots hastened to give their children new revolutionary names as well. There were many Roses and Jacinthes among the girls, but at republican baptisms, no one flinched at such names as Chiendent Pluviôse (chiendent is a weed), Clover, Rosemary, Celery, Clay, Republican, Floréal, Equality, Work, Jemappes, Victory, Brutus, Minerva, Rousseau, Voltaire, Friend of the People. The fashion for revolutionary first names varied, of course, depending on the region. Where Catholic tradition was strong, they were little valued. Games, including chess, were also rearranged. In the first games, the kings became geniuses (of peace, of commerce, of war, and of the arts) and the fallen queens symbolized freedom (of the press, of profession, religious persuasion, of marriage). As for the knaves, they were transformed into sansculottes with orders to promote equality of rank, race, law, and duty.

Watchcases with revolutionary motifs.

Sansculotte thermometer decorated with the liberty cap, graded in degrees of centigrade.

Lauros-Giraudon

The Press

"The business done by the merchants of Paris is making incredible strides. I went to the Palais-Royal to see some new publications. Each hour brings a new one. Today, which is June 9, 1789, thirteen have appeared; yesterday there were sixteen, and last week, ninety-two! The passion for reading political writings is growing everywhere. The great majority is favorable to liberty and violently opposed to the clergy and the nobility." Thus wrote an Englishman who was passing through Paris at the beginning of the Revolution.

With the Declaration of the Rights of Man and of the Citizen, which recognized freedom of the press, newspapers proliferated. In 1791 there were no fewer than 150 newspapers in Paris alone. Some were temporary and disappeared after a few weeks or even days. Others, like Prudhomme and Loustalot's Les Révolutions de Paris ("The Revolutions of Paris") and Hébert's Le Père Duchesne ("Father Duchesne"), enjoyed great popularity in sansculotte circles and reached a large number of printings.

Until the fall of the monarchy, the royalist press had flourished as well as the revolutionary one. In La Chronique Scandaleuse ("Scandalous Chronicles"), and then in Les Actes des Apôtres ("The Acts of the Apostles"), Rivarol ridiculed republican patriots. Sometimes, as in Le Contre-Poison ("The Antidote to Poison"), the Sottises de la Semaine ("The Week's Nonsense"), or Le Véritable Ami de la Reine ("The Queen's True Friend"), the tone was sharp and ironic: "Have the democrats stolen your cabbages, your carrots, your turnips, and your onions? Fine! Be happy about it. Have they tried you unfairly and you lost? Fine! Be happy about it. Have they taken your clothes and your money? Oh! This time rejoice! They've taken your cows and your mules? Just fine! Finance is ruined, murders are rife, altars upturned, honest people slandered and hanged? Rejoice, for we are free!"

No one was squeamish about giving false information or making a travesty of the truth. One counterrevolutionary described the Festival of the Federation as follows: "There were at least fifteen hundred souls [in reality, there were 400,000

LA BOUCHE DE FER

... Linguae centum sunt, oculi centum, oraque oentum, AENEID. Ferrea vox.

Nᵒ. I, publié le 10 Octob. 1790. 2ᵉ. Année.

Le cercle social, qui surveille et dirige la Bouche de fer, journal patriotique et fraternel, a pour objet, dans cet ouvrage,

LA CONFÉDÉRATION UNIVERSELLE DES AMIS DE LA VÉRITÉ.

Mais, dans une entreprise d'une aussi haute importance que le manifeste d'un pacte fédératif, il est indispensable de se borner long-temps à la spéculation, avant de descendre à une application pratique : car voulez-vous savoir pourquoi, dans l'interprétation des loix sociales et naturelles on avance peu ou presque point, depuis tant de siècles ? Pourquoi toujours, après tant de fatigues, on se retrouve au point d'où l'on est parti ? C'est que toujours on se décide avant un mûr examen; c'est que toujours on établit en principes ce qui n'est encore qu'en question; c'est que toujours on

A

Nᵒ. 1.

(67)

Nᵒ. VIII.

JOURNAL DU CLUB DES CORDELIERS.

SOCIÉTÉ DES AMIS DES DROITS DE L'HOMME ET DU CITOYEN.

dix-neuf juillet 1791.

Après la lecture du procès-verbal, la société a entendu le rapport d'un de ses membres relativement aux quatre compagnons chapeliers emprisonnés à la conciergerie, et sur lesquels seuls le glaive de la loi paroissoit vouloir s'appésantir, quoiqu'ils fussent précisément les moins coupables, et ceux qui avoient montré le plus de modération et de sagesse, lors de la malheureuse dispute qui fut la cause de l'incarcération de seize d'entreux. La société prenant en considération les vexations dont il est à craindre que ces malheureux deviennent victimes, a nommé quatre commissaires pour se rendre à la mairie, et requérir la liberté provisoire de ces citoyens.

people] who went home all muddied, after the oath-taking. Carra, a friend of Robespierre, said audibly that the rain was an attack from heaven." One day in 1793, the Feuille du matin ("Morning Paper") stated that a certain tavern was offering its clients human flesh, since "the scrofulous Marat" had gone there to "get drunk."

The patriotic press, which espoused radically different ideas, flourished, too. Among the papers were Le Point du Jour ("Daybreak") by Bigorre, Les Annales Patriotiques ("Patriotic Annals") by Carra and Mercier, and Le Patriote Francais ("French Patriot") by Brissot. Since they were politicians as well as journalists, the authors of these sheets wanted at one and the same time to present the news, defend their point of view, and draw their readers into supporting the Revolution. Thus, in the days preceding October 5 and 6, 1789, Les Révolutions de Paris warned the people, "Let us be on our guard! We need a renewal of the Revolution!" Marat, in L'Ami du Peuple ("The People's Friend"), openly called for the sansculottes to massacre the detainees in the prisons in September 1792!

As the Revolution grew progressively more violent, the tone of the newspapers grew more provocative. Hébert created Le Père Duchesne ("Father Duchesne"), an often vulgar, truculent character who, in the imaginary dialogues that he conducted with the great persons of the times and in the humorous articles that Marat had this fictional character write, summed up all the enthusiasm and anger of the people of Paris. For instance, after August 10, 1792, he said, "What are we going to do with the wretched great pig [the king] that has cost us so much to fatten?" When the revolutionaries began gathering metal for the war effort, he proclaimed, "Down with bells! We're finished with bells bursting our eardrums. They're going to stop annoying the living in order to produce money and cannon."

So that Parisians could read their newspapers, the workers in some hundred printing shops in the capital worked in shifts, day and night. The presses printed sheet after sheet. On some days when some great event was taking place, crowds of readers lined up in front of the shops and fought over the first copies, which had not even had time to dry.

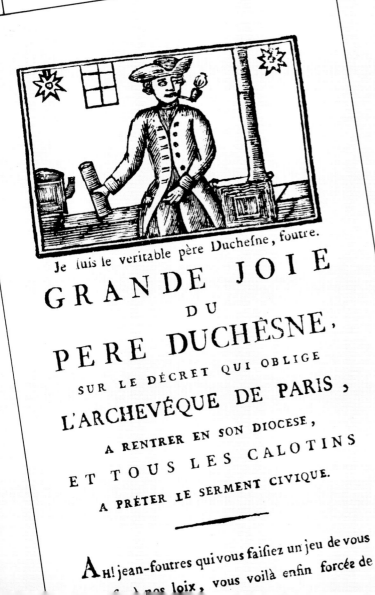

Je fuis le veritable père Duchefne, foutre.

GRANDE JOIE
DU
PERE DUCHÊSNE,
SUR LE DÉCRET QUI OBLIGE
L'ARCHEVÊQUE DE PARIS,
A RENTRER EN SON DIOCESE,
ET TOUS LES CALOTINS
A PRÊTER LE SERMENT CIVIQUE.

AH! jean-foutres qui vous faifiez un jeu de vous
des loix, vous voilà enfin forcée de

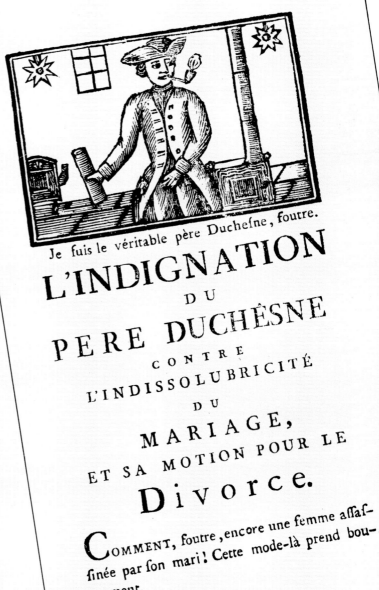

Je fuis le véritable père Duchefne, foutre.

L'INDIGNATION
DU
PERE DUCHÊSNE
CONTRE
L'INDISSOLUBRICITÉ
DU
MARIAGE,
ET SA MOTION POUR LE
Divorce.

COMMENT, foutre, encore une femme affaf-
finée par fon mari! Cette mode-là prend bou-
grement.

The Death of Danton

After some weeks of absence in autumn 1793, Danton returned to Paris to condemn the politics of the Enragés. He believed that with the fall of Hébert, the Reign of Terror would end. The federalist revolt had been crushed, the Vendée subdued, and the frontiers safeguarded, thanks to the valiant soldiers of Year II. So why go on spilling blood?

Danton gathered around him the Indulgents, who stated their ideas in *Le Vieux Cordelier* (*The Old Cordelier*), the newspaper of Desmoulins, a friend of Robespierre and one of the men of July 14.

In the committees, however, supporters of the Reign of Terror were in the majority. They held against Danton his popularity and the airs he gave himself. They saw him as a self-confident, arrogant giant who enjoyed and took advantage of every kind of pleasure and who stood in clear contrast to the stiff respectability demonstrated by Robespierre, the Incorruptible.

"We shall get rid of this great stuffed turbot," promised Voulland of the Committee of Public Safety. Jean-Marie Collot d'Herbois, less given to gastronomic metaphors, was just as sinister: "We shall certainly find a way to lead him to the scaffold along with others who think like him!"

Robespierre knew what the Revolution owed to Danton. Hadn't he formed the committees and the Revolutionary Tribunal, whose clemency he was asking for now? "Do you want to hang our best patriots?" Robespierre asked those who now attacked the man who had roused the nation with his speech saying "The country is in danger. . . ."

Saint-Just, however, succeeded in changing Robespierre's mind. He pointed out that friends of Danton, among them Fabre d'Églantine (author of the republican calendar), had made money by encouraging the sale of the assets of the India Company (an overseas trading corporation founded by the Bourbon minister Charles-Alexandre Calonne) to big business.

At the Convention on 11 *Germinal* (March 31, 1794), Saint-Just read a report accusing Danton of being at once a thief, a traitor, and even a royalist! Arrested that same day, Danton tried to use his trial to unmask his accusers. "Posterity must at least know that we were not thieves!" Addressing Joseph Cambon, administrator of the national finances, who had come to testify against him, Danton asked, "Well, Cambon, do you believe I'm guilty?" Embarrassed, Cambon smiled. "You see, he's laughing; he doesn't believe it," cried Danton. "Write it down, clerk, that he's laughing!"

Danton was not allowed to summon any witnesses. So, he bellowed, "If my denunciators were here, I would confound them in front of the people and I would be generous enough to ask for their pardon. Let them lead me to death. I shall sleep in glory. Soon I shall be domiciled in nothingness, with my name in the Pantheon! I, the protector of the royalists? Men of my stamp cannot be bought!" Furious, he predicted: "The people will tear my enemies to shreds within three months!" The public applauded. Herman, the president of the Tribunal, had the room cleared.

On 14 *Germinal* (April 3, 1794), Danton tore the indictment apart point by point. It contained not a shade of proof. The next day the hearing began late. Outraged, Fouquier-Tinville wrote to the Committee of Public Safety, "A terrible storm is threatening. The accused are calling on all the people. . . . The only way out of it would be a decree of

'removed from the proceedings.'" And that's what took place. Claiming that Danton was directing a plot against the Republic from the depths of his cell, the Convention authorized the Tribunal to sit in the absence of the accused.

Before being excluded from the proceedings, Danton had time to declare: "Look at these cowardly assassins, they will follow us to death itself. Tried without being heard! No debate! That is dictatorship! The dictator has torn off his mask." There was complete chaos; the public howled, and all the accused were led away on the pretext that they had "insulted national justice." All were declared guilty of a "monarchist plot!"

In his cell, Danton talked aloud to himself. "I am leaving everything in a terrible mess. . . . Authority rests with the greatest rogues. . . ." On April 5, in the cart taking him to the scaffold, he shouted, "People, you are being deceived! Your defenders are being massacred!" Passing in front of the house where Robespierre lived, he cried, "You hide in vain, Robespierre! You will follow me! Your house will be razed! Salt will be sown there!"

Arriving at the scaffold, which he was the last to mount that day, he looked the executioner, Sansom, in the eye and said, "Do not forget, be sure not to forget, to show my head to the people! It is well worth seeing!"

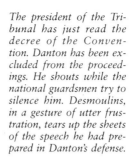

The president of the Tribunal has just read the decree of the Convention. Danton has been excluded from the proceedings. He shouts while the national guardsmen try to silence him. Desmoulins, in a gesture of utter frustration, tears up the sheets of the speech he had prepared in Danton's defense.

Revolutionary Festivals

By means of various festivals throughout the Revolution, the French enjoyed celebrating their new regime, their military victories, their great leaders, and the ideals for which they fought.

From 1790 on, the peasants, believing themselves now freed of all taxes, set up maypoles (trees or posts decorated with garlands and bouquets of flowers), symbols of liberty around which the villagers gathered to rejoice. Sometimes the rejoicings were accompanied by violence, either real or symbolic. It was not uncommon to see peasants enter the village church to tear out the seats reserved there for the nobility and to make a large bonfire of them. On a maypole in the Cahors region could be read: "This post is to establish the liberty of France and the happiness of all good citizens, and to hang aristocrats."

In Paris, after the unanimous enthusiasm generated by the Festival of the Federation, festivals became real political manifestations, where differing opinions were expressed on the future of the Revolution. The moderate middle classes organized gatherings that were occasions for parading the National Guard and the regiments whose duty it was to suppress any attempt at a popular uprising. The sansculottes responded by honoring, in their imposing processions, those patriots who had been assassinated by royalists and to whom they were devotedly attached, such as Marat, who was stabbed on July 13, 1793.

But with the coming of the revolutionary government and of the Reign of Terror, festivals were no longer left to the initiative of single groups. They became official gatherings. Men, women, and children were summoned to take part. Their instructions went even as far as arrangements for each person's costume and headdress. Absentees and people who did not seem to be showing enough enthusiasm were subject to heavy penalties.

In the spring of 1794, Robespierre commissioned the painter Jacques-Louis David to organize a festival of the Supreme Being.

A disciple of the philosopher Rousseau, Robespierre, who was a Deist, not a Christian, had decided on this celebration to mark his hostility to both Catholics and atheists alike.

On the morning of 20 *Prairial* year II (June 8, 1794), all the streets and houses, decorated with garlands and oak leaves, were swarming with people. A crowd of 500,000 people moved gradually into the Champ de Mars, where an artificial mountain had been raised and topped by a tree of liberty and flanked by a column bearing a statue to the genius of the French people. The statue held the symbols of liberty and equality. Everything was ready to welcome an extraordinary procession coming from the Convention. At its head marched a company of gunners, followed by young girls dressed in white. The girls were followed by a heavy chariot drawn by eight oxen with gilded horns. On the chariot was a woman who symbolized abundance; she was surrounded by piles of fruit and wheat sheaves. Citizens and their wives, serious and serene, and laced with tricolor ribbons representing wisdom and virtue, moved forward in their turn as an orchestra played a hymn to the Supreme Being.

Walking a few steps ahead of the other members of the Convention, Robespierre held a bouquet of flowers and ears of wheat. In the midst of ovations, he went toward a papier-mâché statue that represented atheism and set it on fire. As it burned, it revealed the statue of the goddess of reason, who was quite blackened by the smoke.

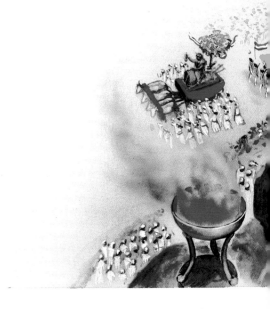

Robespierre then climbed the steps leading to the summit of the "mountain." An orchestra and choirs intoned the hymn to "the Father of the Universe." At each verse, cries of "Long live the Republic" resounded, and at the last couplet a tremendous salvo of cannons thundered out and put an end to the festival.

The Incorruptible seemed to be at the height of his power, but during the ceremony he had heard gibes spreading through the ranks of the deputies of the Convention. One of the sansculottes had even snarled: "The pig, he's not satisfied with being master, he has to be God Himself!" On this day of seeming glory for him, Robespierre had made new enemies. Perhaps he realized this when he confided that very evening, "My friends, you will not see me much longer. . . ."

9 Thermidor

With Danton and the Indulgents eliminated, nothing seemed to stand in the way of Robespierre. The Incorruptible had nothing but friends in the committees. Yet, at the Committee of Public Safety, the atmosphere had continued to deteriorate. In permanent session, sleeping less than three hours a night and hardly eating, these men exhausted themselves from meeting to meeting, whether they were members of the Convention or Jacobins. Each one, believing he was doing his best to bring triumph to the Revolution, took criticism badly and was prone to accuse anyone of being a traitor who did not share his point of view.

At the Committee of Public Safety on June 15, 1794, Robespierre denounced the excesses of the politics of terror used by Fouché and Jean-Lambert Tallien in Lyons and Bordeaux, where they were representatives on mission. He demanded that they

be tried. Billaud-Varenne and Collot d'Herbois, who blamed Robespierre for having stopped dechristianization and for having organized the Festival of the Supreme Being, refused to back him up. As a sign of protest, Robespierre stayed away from the meetings of the Committee of Public Safety and no longer left home except to defend his policies at the Jacobin Club, where he had dependable friends, as well as enemies who accused him of wanting to set up a dictatorship.

At the Convention, Tallien and Fouché, along with Vadier, president of the Committee of General Security, circulated among the deputies lists of the accused, insinuating that Robespierre wanted to have everyone on the list executed. Having determined to explain his instructions to the Convention, Robespierre appeared on 8 *Thermidor* (July 26, 1794). He mounted the platform and denounced the "mischief makers." "We must," he said, "renovate the Committee of General Security and purge the Committee of Public Safety." Fearing for their lives, the deputies were silent. Cambon, the administrator of national finances, finally broke the silence. "One man alone is paralyzing the Convention, and that man is Robespierre!" Another voice grew bold enough to say, "Have the courage to name those you accuse!" "Name them!" "Name them!" The room took up the challenge. But Robespierre named no one; he understood that the Convention was now hostile toward him.

However, at the Jacobin Club, the majority supported Robespierre. That evening, in the meeting room of the Committee of Public Safety, Saint-Just was writing nervously when Collot d'Herbois said to him, "Are you preparing our indict-ment?" Saint-Just replied, "Yes, you're right, I'm preparing yours."

The next day, 9 *Thermidor*, Saint-Just tried in vain to denounce Billaud-Varenne, Fouché, and Tallien before the Convention. The Assembly booed him. Robespierre asked to be heard. "Down with the tyrant!" they howled from the benches. Collot d'Herbois, who was presiding over the session, rang his bell furiously to drown out the voices of the accusers. Amid shouts and tumult, the Convention voted to arrest Robespierre, Saint-Just, and Couthon. Augustin, Robespierre's younger brother, and Le Bas demanded "the honor of being arrested, too."

The accused were put in different prisons, but no jailer would agree to shut up Robespierre. The news spread quickly around the city's districts. The sansculottes soon freed the prisoners, who took refuge in the town hall, under the protection of the Commune. However, the three thousand men from the districts, tired of waiting without receiving any orders, gradually abandoned their posts. At two-thirty in the morning, the National Guards were dispatched from the Convention to the room where the five prisoners were gathered. Le Bas shot himself with one bullet through the head, and Robespierre's jaw was fractured. (Had he wanted to commit suicide?) Augustin Robespierre, believing his brother to be dead, jumped through the window and was badly hurt. That evening twelve followers of Robespierre went to the scaffold without having been tried. Couthon, paralyzed and in a wheelchair, was almost cut to pieces by the crowd. The executioners went so far as to guillotine the corpse of Le Bas. This torture took place to the satisfaction of many bourgeoisie and in the face of indifference on the part of much of the Parisian populace.

Along with Robespierre, the Revolution of the people died. The Incorruptible, foreseeing his end, had said on 8 *Thermidor*, "What friend of the country would want to survive the moment when he is no longer allowed to serve it or to defend oppressed innocence?"

On 10 Thermidor, *at two-thirty in the morning, Paul de Barras, at the head of the national guardsmen who were faithful to the Convention, entered the town hall. The procession carried away Robespierre, lying on a litter. Saint-Just followed him. Two guards dragged out the corpse of Le Bas, who had just killed himself.*

Is the Revolution Over?

On the morning after the death of Robespierre, Emmanuel Sièyes, a deputy speaking at the Convention, expressed in one short sentence the feeling of relief felt by most of the country. "I have lived through it!" Wasn't that the main thing?

The Plain (the moderates), now in charge of the Assembly, initiated a reaction to the Terror that surpassed anything the enemies of the Incorruptible had imagined as they were organizing his downfall. The Revolutionary Tribunal acquitted most of the suspects imprisoned between 1793 and July 1794, but it condemned to death Carrier and Fouquier-Tinville, who were responsible for the excesses of the Terror.

The Committee of Public Safety lost all power, and the Revolutionary Tribunal was suppressed in 1795. Freed from censorship, the press attacked the Jacobins with virulence as well as irony. In *La Quotidienne* (*"The Daily Newspaper"*), the following dialogue could be read: "You will agree that all Jacobins are not scoundrels? Yes, but you will agree that scoundrels are all Jacobins!"

Former terrorists, like Tallien and Barras, allied themselves with escaped Girondists and even with royalists, who were again raising their heads, delighted not to have lost them after all. They gathered in bands of *muscadins* ("dandies"), an appellation earned by their affectations and extravagant dress. (A *muscadin* was, at the time, the name for a little sugar candy.) These dandies frequented the cafés of the Palais-Royal, proclaiming loudly and emphatically that they hated the Revolution. Armed with canes that they called their "executive power," they chased anything resembling a sansculotte.

The Convention closed down the Jacobin Club after November 1794. On 4 *Nivôse* (December 24) it ended the general price controls. Prices shot up and reduced the poverty-stricken to begging. The profiteers benefited from the fortunes they had accumulated by selling materiel, feed, and horses to the army, and by buying up national property at very low prices.

In Paris these nouveaux riches, who had been constrained by fear of the Incorruptible, now flaunted their wealth in loud, expensive dress. The restaurants were never empty. The theaters put on plays at which the public applauded uproariously every time mention was made of the fallen monarchy. The number of public balls multiplied. The most popular was the "victims' ball," reserved for relatives of the guillotined. It was good form for men to go to it dressed in mourning and for women to wear little red ribbons around their necks!

The salon of Madame Tallien, a former actress whose husband had saved her from Robespierre's prisons, attracted artists and men of politics. They christened her "Our Lady of *Thermidor*."

The sansculottes tried to react. On 1 *Prairial* year III (May 20, 1795), they came from the *faubourgs* ("popular districts") and invaded the Convention, crying for "Bread! And the Constitution of 1793!" But the National Guard dispersed them. The army pursued them into the Faubourg St.-Antoine, where the inhabitants had to give up their arms. From then on, the people were excluded from the Revolution. Not until May 27, 1830, would they take to the streets again.

Taking advantage of the Convention's indulgence, many émigrés came back to France and were welcomed and protected by the royalists, who displayed their con-

victions without risk since the Committees of Surveillance had been suppressed. The royalists even hoped to restore the monarchy and place the late king's young son on the throne. But the death of the dauphin Louis XVII (June 8, 1795) deprived them of their sovereign. So they centered their hopes on the two brothers of Louis XVI, the future Louis XVIII and Charles X.

On October 26, 1795, the Convention dispersed after adopting a new constitution. This constitution suppressed universal suffrage and granted voting rights to only twenty thousand electors, who were charged with electing and renewing annually the two assemblies: the Council of the Five Hundred and the Council of the Elders. These councils were supposed to represent the people in the new regime, the Directory, so called because the government would be led by five directors.

The rich young people who frequented the gardens of the Palais-Royal during the day and the salons and balls at night launched an extravagant fashion. The incroyables ("dandies") dressed as differently as possible from the sansculottes: they wore pointed shoes; silk stockings; breeches in the mode of the old regime; and long coats pinched in at the waist, with collars so exaggerated they reached above the ears. Their necks were bundled in enormous cravats. They wore cocked hats so large that they hid the face. Their feminine counterparts, the ultra-fashionable merveilleuses, dressed in light voiles in the antique mode. They had their own language and tried not to pronounce the r, as in roi ("king") because they seemed to deplore the king's death. They said ma paole for parole, meaning "word"; c'est hoîble for horrible; supême for suprême; meveilleux for merveilleux, meaning "marvelous"; and sexa for qu'est-ce que c'est que ça meaning "what's that?"

Bonaparte, Commander in Chief

Napoléon Bonaparte, son of a Corsican gentleman, was only twenty years old when the Revolution broke out. He was then a lieutenant in the royal army, having completed courses at the military school at Brienne-le-Chateau. Helped by his talent for strategy and his republican convictions, the events of the Revolution allowed him to advance his career rapidly. In 1793 he was promoted to captain and distinguished himself at the siege of Toulon, which the royalists had opened to the British and the patriots had retaken on December 18. Thanks to this victory, which was largely due to him, plus the friendship of Augustin Robespierre, Napoléon was made a general the next year, at the age of twenty-four!

Regarded as a Jacobin linked with Robespierre, Napoléon was arrested after 9 *Thermidor* and imprisoned at the fort of Antibes. It was several months before he regained his liberty and his rank. Back in Paris and a general without troops, he was dying of boredom after refusing a command in the Vendée. Soon, however, he was offered a chance to distinguish himself once more in the service of the Republic. In October 1795 a royalist conspiracy broke out. Barras, Commander-in-Chief of the army of the Interior, called on Napoléon to suppress the uprising. On 13 *Vendémiaire* (October 5) the young general pointed his cannon at the Church of St.-Roch, where the insurgents were preparing for action. As insurgents emerged, bullets and cannon shot gave them no chance. It was a massacre.

At the beginning of 1796, France was still at war with Great Britain and Austria. To conquer the Austrians, Carnot, one of the five directors, decided to launch three armies in the direction of Vienna. Two were to pass through Germany while the third would create a diversion in Italy, then occupied by the Austrians.

On March 26 in Nice, Napoléon took command of the army that was to cross the Alps and penetrate into Italy. Under his command were thirty-six thousand poorly equipped men dressed in rags, most of them marching barefoot. But the regiments were courageous, seasoned by the preceding campaigns and capably led by good officers. Napoléon understood that his army must get into the war quickly and live off

the country it was invading, points he made in a speech to his men: "Soldiers, you are naked . . . I am about to lead you into the most fertile plains in the world. Rich provinces and large cities will be in your power; you will find there honor, glory, and riches. . . ."

Under the worst of conditions, the army of Italy crossed the Alpine passes in a few days, and within two weeks it had conquered the Piedmont. In May, Napoléon occupied Milan, where he settled in like a real sovereign before pushing his conquest toward the south. He took Bologna and Leghorn and was welcomed triumphantly in Florence. Without asking the Directory's opinion, he installed vassal governments of France everywhere. He subjected Italy to systematic pillaging, ransacked the overrun cities, and snatched a considerable fortune from the churches and palazzos, which he divided among his soldiers, officers, and his own family.

The Italian republicans and Jacobins, who had welcomed the French as liberators, were disenchanted. They began to realize that their country was nothing but a prize of war for Napoléon. He gained popularity for himself by having the French press publish a continuing recital of battles, in which the young general was portrayed as a courageous patriot (which he was) and a disinterested one, too (which was certainly less true!).

In January 1797, Napoléon won a decisive battle at Rivoli against the Austrians, who were forced to evacuate Italy prior to signing a peace agreement with France some months later. But France was still at war with its most formidable adversary, Great Britain.

Having estimated that a landing on the shores of England would be impossible, the Directory accepted Napoléon's proposal to conquer Egypt, crossroads of the trade between Great Britain and its Indian empire. Eluding the vigilant British squadrons, three hundred vessels put ashore a powerful French army on the coast of Egypt. On July 21, 1798, the formidable Mameluke Cavalry was crushed by Napoléon's troops. But on August 1 the British fleet destroyed all the French ships anchored in the roadstead of Abukir. Napoléon's army was a prisoner of its own conquest.

After having led his soldiers into Palestine, where they fought some more famous battles (Nazareth, Mount Tabor) that also served his propaganda purposes in France, Napoléon had to retreat toward Egypt. He left his army in Egypt under the command of General Jean-Baptiste Kléber and sailed for France, where a new destiny awaited him.

18 Brumaire

1799. For four years the Directory had been confronting endless difficulties. For a long time, assignats had not been worth anything, and their replacement in 1796 by another kind of paper money (territorial money orders) had not relieved the situation. Functionaries could survive only by selling their services and influence to the highest bidder. Corruption was widespread. Economic activity slackened. Bands of brigands were said to be roaming all over the country.

In the west, civil war broke out again in 1795. The Chouans (Breton royalists) even occupied several important cities for a time. However, an attempt to land royalist troops composed of émigrés on Quiberon Peninsula failed completely.

In Paris there were attempts from all sides to bring down the Directory. In 1796 the regime had to deal with the "conspiracy of the equals," a plot led by Gracchus Babeuf, who wanted to establish an egalitarian republic and abolish private property. Each year the assemblies (the Elders and the Five Hundred) were renewed by elections. The majorities were constantly changing. Sometimes the royalists dominated and wanted to eliminate the former Jacobins; sometimes the latter returned to power and threatened to resume the politics of terror applied under Robespierre. The Directory could only keep itself alive by rescinding the election results!

Discontent became more and more widespread throughout the country. The Directory was bankrupt. It had to forego paying two thirds of its debts, and it reintroduced town dues as well as taxes on transportation and wines, just as in the time of the king. In Paris two of the directors, Sieyés and Ducos; some ministers, Fouché and Talleyrand; and some bankers and businessmen were ready to topple the regime. They needed a leader, a prestigious and not too scrupulous general, who would assure the support of the army, which was indispensable to the success of a coup d'etat. After they had examined several possibilities, the conspirators chose Napoléon, who had just returned to Paris, having left his army in Egypt. Their choice seemed even more appropriate, for Lucien, Napoléon's brother, was then president of the Council of the Five Hundred. The coup was quickly organized.

On 18 *Brumaire* (November 9, 1799) one of the conspirators circulated the rumor that some soldiers were threatening Paris; false witnesses even testified that they had seen them some leagues from the capital. The two assemblies (the Elders and the Five Hundred) decided to take shelter in the château of St.-Cloud, meanwhile entrusting to Napoléon Bonaparte the duty of defending Paris!

The next day at St.-Cloud, the deputies observed that the château was surrounded by Napoléon's troops. Realizing that they had fallen into a trap, the Five Hundred swore an oath of fidelity to the Constitution and vowed not to yield to force.

Napoléon decided to hurry things along. He pushed himself forcibly into the *Orangerie* (the orange-tree greenhouse), where the Council of Five Hundred was meeting. His brusque arrival caused an incredible uproar. Deputies surrounded him, jostled him; one took him by the collar, and others howled: "Down with the dictator! Outlaw! Long live the Constitution!" Livid with rage and surprised at such a reaction, Napoléon could not utter a word. His grenadiers had to rescue him from the fury of the deputies. In the scuffle he had been lightly scratched; there were drops of blood on his face.

The situation seemed to be in jeopardy for the conspirators, but Lucien Bonaparte restored it in a few moments. He came out of the château, mounted his horse, and harangued his brother's soldiers, showing them their general "wounded by the daggers of the deputies." To the sound of a drum and with bayonets ready, the solders broke into the meeting room. Hampered by the red capes of their uniforms, the deputies fled, jumping out of the windows and disappearing into the park. The woods were searched, and some of the deputies, a minority, were brought back. Faced with threats, they agreed to vote for the end of the Directory and to nominate three consuls—Napoléon, Sieyés, and Ducos—with orders to draw up a new constitution. For Napoléon Bonaparte a march to power began that would, in 1804, make him the emperor of a France that had guillotined its king eleven years earlier.

A Parisian woman told the story of the coup d'etat in her diary: "The reconciliation between Sieyés and Bonaparte was no longer secret, and we knew that both would unite their efforts and pull the country out of the gulf it was sliding into. . . . As I write, the two councils are meeting at St.-Cloud. . . . There will be no lack of speeches at the session of the Five Hundred, but the orators will soon find that their words carry no farther than the sound of their voices. . . . Such measures were imposed of necessity, if France was not to be left rolling in the abyss. . . . [They] revive the courage of honest people . . . inspire confidence abroad."

How the Revolution Changed France

For ten years the Revolution tried to change French life profoundly. Some of its decrees and laws took hold immediately, but others took decades to implant themselves or to be properly applied.

In 1889, France celebrated the centenary of the Revolution in a fitting manner. With this poster the municipality of Corbeil, in Essonne, informed its inhabitants of the program of celebrations.

The Departments

The departments were created by the Constituent Assembly on February 26, 1790, to simplify the incredible administrative complexity of France under the old regime. The country had been divided into provinces, districts, bailliages, dioceses, and so on. To trace the boundaries of each department and to determine the number of departments, a simple principle was applied: no place in the department would be farther than a day's journey by horseback from any other place in the same department. The departments were originally eighty-three in number and reached 130 in 1810, after the conquests of the Republic and the Empire.

The Metric System

Still in the same spirit of simplification and of rationalization, the Convention instituted the metric system for weights, measures, and monetary units by a law of 18 *Germinal* year III (April 8, 1794). Thus the liter, the gram, the meter, the unit of 100 square meters, the cubic meter, and the franc were established. Decades passed, however, before the habit of using the new system caught on, so firmly anchored was the everyday use of words like *pint, pound, yard,* and *yardstick.*

Michel Pierre

The Jury

Before the Revolution, justice was handed down by judges who had absolute power to condemn or to declare a suspect innocent. In 1790 the Constituent Assembly instituted the use of juries composed of citizens drawn by lot, who met in the case of trials to deliver justice alongside the judges.

Divorce

Legal rupture of marriage, which until then had been considered indissoluble, was introduced in France by a law on September 20, 1792. (This law was suppressed in 1816 but reinstated in 1884.)

Paper Money

The assignat was the first real paper money in the history of France. With the national property as security, the first assignats were well accepted, but the *planche à billets*, or "printing plate for bills," was used too often, and the bills depreciated, reviving the suspicions of the French people about the bills' real worth. Only in 1802 did confidence return, when Napoléon decided to create paper money that was convertible to gold.

Universal Suffrage

For the first time in the history of France, universal suffrage was instituted to elect the Convention in September 1792. However, it excluded domestic servants and women from the right to vote; they did not obtain this elementary right until 1945, more than a century and a half after the Revolution!

In a more anecdotal manner, we also owe to the Revolution the first great national exhibition, organized under the directors in 1798, in which the main products of craft and industry of the period were shown. Among the inventions owed to this era and that gave promise of a great future was the parachute, invented by Gamerin in 1797. He jumped from a balloon in a wicker basket suspended from a great open bag of cloth. Let us remember, too, the initiation of the first matrimonial agencies by citizen Liardot, who also published twice a week the *Marriage Indicator*, in which "all the unattached hearts of the Republic" were listed!

Joseph-Ignace Guillotin (1738–1814), a doctor and deputy of the Third Estate in 1789, became the promoter of a "separating machine" meant to shorten the suffering of the condemned. During a speech to the Constituent Assembly on December 11, he was able to convince his colleagues of the usefulness of a machine that would henceforth bear his name. He later despaired when he realized the excessive use that was being made of it.

The Victims of the Revolution

In all, the Reign of Terror claimed fifty thousand victims. From the seventeen thousand names of those condemned to death, to which must be added many anonymous victims in Lyons and Nantes, the historians have constructed some statistics

The western provinces, affected by the wars of the Vendée and the Chouan uprising, and the departments of the Rhône—the Bouches-du-Rhône and the Var—affected by the counter-revolution, counted respectively fifty-one percent and nineteen percent of the victims. Paris, where the Revolutionary Tribunal tried not only the detainees of the capital city but also suspects from the provinces, counted sixteen percent. The Great Terror that followed the decrees of 22 *Prairial* Year II was confined to Paris during June and July of 1794. The provincial judges seem to have been less bloodthirsty. Six departments had no victims whatsoever, and thirty-one departments had fewer than ten.

Why were they guillotined?
In seventy-eight percent of cases, judgment was pronounced for rebellion and treason; in ten percent for "federalism" (this was the case of the condemned in Lyons); and in nine percent simply because of opinions that were held.

Who was guillotined?
Even though they were the principal players, artisans and shopkeepers paid the heaviest price to the Revolution; they filled thirty-one percent of the carts carrying the condemned to the guillotine. The peasants, twenty-eight percent, were mainly Vendéans. Priests represented seven percent, and the nobility about eight percent. The rest were other religious people, politicians, or did not fit into these categories

The Famous guillotine victims
Besides the politicians, the nobility, and the clergy, the executioner cut off the heads of Madame du Barry, Louis XV's favorite; of the chemist Antoine Lavoisier who was also in the Farmers General; of Fabre d'Églantine, a poet who was a friend of Danton; and of André Chenier, the poet who on his way to the scaffold struck his brow and said, "And yet, I had something in there!"

The war resulted in nine times more deaths than the Reign of Terror. In ten years, France lost two percent of its population.

CIVI OPTIMO

Quid verum atque decens curo et rogo, et omnis in hoc sum

PETITION

J. I. GUILLOTIN

Docteur-Régent, ancien Professeur de la Faculté de Médecine de Paris.

Né à Saintes.

Medico peritissimo, amico   Offer. Addictiß. CHEREAU.

They Made the Revolution

MAXIMILIEN de ROBESPIERRE

Born in 1758 in Arras, Maximilien de Robespierre was the son of a lawyer who belonged to a very old family of gentlemen of the law. Orphaned at a very young age (his mother died when he was six and his father, crazed with grief, abandoned his children and disappeared into Germany), he was raised by his maternal grandfather. Sensitive and intelligent, the child studied with the Oratorians and made good progress.

Noticed by the bishop of the diocese, he was given a grant to study at the prestigious College of Louis-le-Grand in Paris. There he discovered the writings of the philosophers Montesquieu, Diderot, and especially Rousseau, who became his master in philosophy. He showed himself to be a brilliant student whose qualities were recognized symbolically when he was chosen to recite a speech of welcome to Louis XVI on the king's visit to the college.

In 1781, having received his license in law, Robespierre went back to Arras to enter the legal profession. Life there was difficult. Clients were few, in spite of his fine work in 1783, when he defended a townsman who was accused of witchcraft for having installed a lightning conductor (an invention of Benjamin Franklin) on his roof. Other trials gave him an opportunity to oppose the privileges of the nobility and clergy, and the right of some of his contemporaries to withhold information.

Michel Pierre

Having become better known, and respected by the progressives, he was elected to the Estates General on April 26, 1789, as deputy of the Third Estate for the district of Artois. At the Constituent Assembly, Robespierre attracted attention because of his initiative. He was one of the few to demand universal suffrage, free and obligatory education, taxes on revenue, and a whole collection of measures that made him the hero of many revolutionaries. Even so, people poked fun at his studied manner, his ever-powdered coiffure, his elegant coats, his disagreeable accent, and his long, boring speeches.

Slowly, with his implacable logic and steadfastness, Robespierre came to play an eminent role. Orator at the Jacobin Club, deputy of the Convention, member of the Committee of Public Safety, he became, as he himself wrote, "inflexible toward oppressors because my sympathies are with the oppressed." Having earned the nickname Incorruptible, Robespierre struggled on every front to impose his politics, before succumbing to the blows of a coalition of his enemies on 9 *Thermidor*.

He was guillotined on 10 *Thermidor* Year II (July 28, 1794) and became an almost legendary figure, a symbol of the Reign of Terror for some and of republican principle for others.

They Made the Revolution

GEORGES-JACQUES DANTON

Born in 1759 in Arcis-sur-Aube, Danton was the son of an agent of the law courts and, like Robespierre, studied law. He opened his practice in Paris in 1785. From the very beginning of the Revolution, he called for freedom of the press and of assembly, but he remained close to certain royalist circles until the king's flight to Varennes, when he abandoned the royalists. He played an important role in the fall of the monarchy on August 10, 1792, and became minister of justice at the Convention.

Danton's tall stature, his powerful face, and his talents as an orator all made him one of the revolutionary leaders most admired by the people of Paris. He organized with great determination and skill the resistance of the Prussian invaders (perhaps even by paying Brunswick to evacuate the territory after his defeat at Valmy!). But Danton's taste for pleasure, his friendships with shady businessmen and notorious crooks, and his personal fortune (which accumulated sums of money from all sides) shocked those who wanted the Revolution to be, and remain, a model of virtue and honesty. Among those was his old friend Robespierre, who became more and more hostile toward Danton and, in the end, had him tried, condemned, and finally executed on April 5, 1794.

Michel Pierre

JEAN-PAUL MARAT

Born at Boudry, in the canton of Neuchatel, Switzerland, in 1743, Marat was the son of a Sardinian immigrant. After solid study marked, like Robespierre's, by the philosophical ideas of Rousseau, he became a tutor in a rich Bordeaux family. In 1765 he began a long stay in England, where he attacked in numerous writings the poverty of the humble, the insolence of the rich, and the despotism of the nobles and the clergy. He became a doctor and lived in Scotland, in Holland, and then in Paris, where he became physician to the Comte d'Artois's bodyguards (until 1783) without ever denying his revolutionary ideas.

The events of July 1789 filled Marat with joy, and he founded l'Ami du Peuple ("The People's Friend"), which became one of the most widely read publications in Paris. Once or twice the violence of his articles forced him to take refuge in England, but he returned to France after April 10, 1792, demanding that "the blood of traitors begin to flow." As a Parisian deputy to the Convention, he continued to preach a policy without pardon or leniency toward those he suspected of being hostile to the Revolution. He played a large part in sentencing Louis XVI to death and in the struggle against the Girondists, to whose downfall he contributed in June 1793. On July 13 of the same year, he was assassinated by Charlotte Corday, a young woman who wanted to avenge the deaths of many Girondists. Upon becoming the Martyr of the Revolution, Marat also became a cult figure for the sansculottes, while others rejoiced at the death of the "bloody murderer."

They Made the Revolution

LOUIS-ANTOINE-LÉON de SAINT-JUST

Son of a cavalry officer, Saint-Just was born in 1767 in Decize, in the Nivernais. Eleven years later his family moved to Blérancourt, in Aisne, and he studied at Soissons, then at Rheims, where he earned a law degree. The Revolution filled him with enthusiasm, but he had to wait until 1792, when he reached the required age of 25, to be elected deputy for Aisne at the Convention. There he became the friend of Robespierre, whose stern principles and austere life he shared. In May 1793 he became a member of the Committee of Public Safety, where he promoted the setting up of an authoritarian government based on terror.

Taking the defense of the Republic to heart, Saint-Just had the functionaries, the army suppliers, the officers, and the generals watched by representatives on mission, who had the power of life and death over anyone suspected of incapacity, corruption, or lack of enthusiasm for the Republic. In person he went to the armies of the Rhine and the North, where he put his convictions into practice and exacted a huge contribution from the wealthy citizens of Strasbourg to clothe and equip thousands of ragged soldiers.

Back in Paris, Saint-Just supported Robespierre in his struggle against the Exagérés and the Indulgents. Stubbornly, he prevented Danton and his friends from defending themselves during their trial, thus removing any chance they might have had of escaping the guillotine. To promote a virtuous and heroic republic, he wrote about the education of children. Thus, he promoted state education of boys between the ages of five and sixteen years, and he wished that girls not appear in public unless accompanied by their parents. All were to be brought up "loving silence and brevity."

Faithful to Robespierre until death, Saint-Just was guillotined with him on 10 *Thermidor* (July 28, 1794), having lost none of his terrible cold assurance. He accepted his own death with the same impassivity he had used to bring about that of hundreds of his victims.

CAMILLE DESMOULINS

Son of a lieutenant general in the bailliage of Guise, Camille Desmoulins was born in 1760. Like Robespierre, who became his friend there, he studied on a scholarship at the College of Louis-le-Grand. As a lawyer in Paris, Desmoulins was elected to the Estates General and on July 13, 1789, he harangued the crowd, calling it to arms against the royalists.

As a deputy at the Convention, Desmoulins was not taken seriously, and his talents as an orator were often mocked. It was said of him that he was "a light republican of puns and jokes, a purveyor of cemetery humor."

Desmoulins supported Robespierre in 1792. Then he approached Danton, opposing more and more vigorously the politics of the Terror instigated by the Committee of Public Safety. In his newspaper, *The Old Cordelier,* which began appearing on December 5, 1793, he launched appeals for clemency that irritated Robespierre profoundly. Arrested on March 31, 1794, Desmoulins was tried on the same bench as Danton and his companions. He was guillotined five days later.

Michel Pierre

Glossary

Absolutism   A type of government in which the ruler's power is not restricted in any way.
Aristocracy   Any class that is considered superior because of birth, culture, or wealth.

Bastille   An ancient royal prison in Paris that symbolized tyranny and oppression.
Bourgeoisie   The middle class.

Departments   The administrative regions into which France is divided. Each department elects councils to run the local government.
Despotism   Absolutism.

Émigrés   The nobles and clergy who fled from France during the Revolution to settle in other countries.
Estates-General   French governmental body composed of representatives from the nobility, clergy, and Third Estate. It met in May of 1789 to make decisions concerning the debt and taxes.

Famine   A time when there is a severe shortage of food.
Faubourg   A suburb of a French city.

Guillotine   A device used for execution by beheading.

Livre   An old French coin worth 20 sols.

Monarchy   A government headed by one ruler; generally a king or queen.

National Guard   A citizen militia.

Plague   A dangerous disease that spreads quickly and causes many deaths.
Philosopher   Someone who studies the truth and principles behind all knowledge.

Reign of Terror   The bloodthirsty period between March 1793 and July 1794 when over 17,000 people, thought to be enemies of the Revolution, were put to death.

Salon   A meeting of notable artists, literary figures, or statesmen held at the home of a well-known person.
Sol   An old French coin worth 1/20 of a livre.
Suffrage   The right or privilege of voting.

Third Estate   The common people—those who were not members of the First Estate (the nobility) or the Second Estate (the clergy).
Tocsins   Bells rung as a warning or alarm.

Index

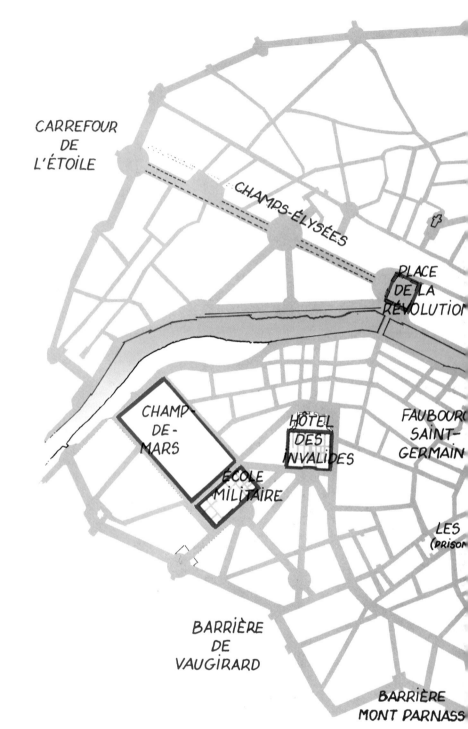

CARREFOUR
DE
L'ÉTOILE

CHAMPS-ÉLYSÉES

PLACE
DE LA
RÉVOLUTION

CHAMP-
DE-
MARS

HÔTEL
DES
INVALIDES

FAUBOURG
SAINT-
GERMAIN

ÉCOLE
MILITAIRE

LES
(PRISON

BARRIÈRE
DE
VAUGIRARD

BARRIÈRE
MONT PARNASS

CARREFOUR
D'ENFER

Revolutionary Paris

When the Revolution began, the city of Paris had just surrounded itself with a new enclosure: the wall of the Farmers General (tax collectors). As its name indicates, the wall was meant to isolate the city from its suburbs so that taxes might be levied on merchandise entering the capital. At each gate the agents of the *Farmers General* inspected the loads and made the transporters pay this tax.

Inside this "wall walling Paris" lived 700,000 people who, in the central districts, were crowded together. However, the people in the suburbs (*faubourgs*), recently included inside the wall, had more spacious houses, often separated by gardens, some of which were as large as fields.

Revolutionary Paris, divided into forty-eight districts in 1790, contained the areas to the west, such as Chaillot and Grenelle, which were still only small villages, plus the suburbs of St.-Honoré and St.-Germain, which were rich quarters, as well as those districts in the center and especially those to the east—the Temple, St.-Antoine, St.-Marceau—which provided the troops of sansculottes who distinguished themselves during the revolution.